Hope

To: A Friend

Sunrise

Encouragement to Overcome

S. R. Adams

Oceanside, California · Dallas, Texas

Unless otherwise noted, Scripture quotations are taken from the King James Version of the Holy Bible.
Other versions used include:
The Holy Bible, New Living Translation, copyright © 1996, 2004, 2007, 2013, 2015 by Tyndale House Foundation. Used by permission of Tyndale House Publishers, Inc., Carol Stream, Illinois 60188. All rights reserved.
The Holy Bible, New International Version copyright ©1973, 1984 by International Bible Society, used by permission of Zondervan Publishing House
S. R. Adams Books, titles, and logos, a letter S combined with the letter R with or without all or part of the company's name, are trademarks of S. R. Adams Brand

S. R. Adams Brand LLC
P. O. Box 2269
Oceanside CA, 92051

ISBN:
978-0-9977465-0-1 (paperback)   978-0-9977465-1-8 (hardcover)
978-0-9977465-3-2 (audio download)   978-0-9977465-2-5 (audiobook)
978-0-9977465-4-9 (e-book)   978-0-9977465-5-6 (CD)
978-0-9977465-6-3 (DVD)

First Edition: July 2016
10 9 8 7 6 5 4 3 2 1

Library of Congress control number   2016910813

Hope To A Friend: Sunrise - Encouragement to overcome /S. R. Adams

Printed in the United States of America

To find out more about the S. R. Adams Brand visit:
www.sradams.com.
Here you can shop, signup for events, view inspirational messages, and more

CONTENTS

Father: Thank you for equipping me, providing for my needs, and making the way

Comforter: Thank you for holding light in darkness

Best Friend: Thank you for showing me the way

Guides & Teachers: Thank you for sharing wisdom

Lights Of The World: Thank you for being you

In Loving Memory of Mommy's
Sky Baby

The heart of a man is a temple

in which the sun rises from and sets again;

with love, it is forever shinning

with forgiveness it entertains hope

S. R. Adams

Introduction

Friends, I've had hard lessons to learn in life. Some lessons, I'm still in the process of learning. Sounds familiar? It should. This is life. We're here to learn. We're here to grow.

For a time, I've sat in darkness. I've dug holes, scratched walls, and knocked down doors to get to where I am now. I've overcome. I've surrendered to change. Now, I sit in darkness watching the sunrise. What a beautiful sight!

I've written this book to guide you through the process of overcoming. I encourage you to find *your* reason to keep on pressing on. Find a reason to arrive at *your* destination no matter the circumstance. Find *your* reason to live.

Life's a journey. It's the process to learning. Living, you'll experience ups and downs. You'll experience change. We're not perfect in this form. My friend, your flesh is to blame; not your spirit. Don't give up on you. Know who you are: let it be your truth. Strive to be a better you: let it be your focus.

I thank *The* Great Spirit for communicating with me; however, I often wonder and ask why. *Why me?* I don't have it all together. I struggle to stay faithful. I struggle to believe. I struggle with addiction. I struggle with fornication. I struggle with fear. I struggle with slothfulness. I struggle with low self-esteem. I struggle to stay sane. Daily, I wrestle with ego. The difference: I refuse to substitute struggle with excuse.

Your *one way now* is not forever. You can't accomplish anything without first living. Learn to fight. Remember, this is your journey. This is your life. You have lessons to learn. My friend, take notes. Lessons are followed by assignment. You will be tested. Life's your teacher. Your purpose is your assignment. You have work to do.

You're not here by chance. You were born to achieve. You were born to become. There's an egg of potential inside of you; developing: to hatch into the world. You've experienced setback, you feel defeated, heartache, pain, disappointment; you've been tempted to give up. You've at some point wanted to wave the white flag. At some point wanted to throw in the towel. No. Don't give up. You're learning how to pass your test. Study to work through the problem. Only those who learn to work through their problems can solve their problems. No worries. When it's time to pass your test: you'll pass the best.

Remember, you're responsible for reaching your destiny. You're responsible for your purpose. It's up to you to become. Do what you're supposed to do: "Study to show thyself approved." Complete the assignment. Nobody's going to do this for you.

My friend, it's not going to be easy. It'll be difficult trying to figure things out. It may not happen when you want it to happen. You might have to lose your mind to find it. You might have to forget who you are: to become who you're supposed to be. At times, you'll be required to let go: to grab hold. You will lose to gain.

I want you to know something, there's two things guaranteed in life: a start, and a finish. You have no control over your start. You don't set your finishing point. Everything in between is up to you. How you cross the finishing line is up to you. If you quit: you're never going to win; you'll never get there; you'll never know if you could pass or not. No. Don't quit! Don't wait! Don't slack! Keep going! Endure! Persevere! Press on! My friend, focus and become. Live your life. Learn the lessons you're to learn. Grow!

Be of good cheer. Don't beat yourself up about it. It's done. Learn from it. Suffer it to be so now. You will not have to sit in darkness much longer. The sun's coming up. It shines at your core. It never goes out. Arise! My friend, "Thy light is come, and the glory of the Lord is risen upon thee."

Take Your Place.

Chapter One:
Bountiful Harvest

You've planted the seeds, now, take cover and let *The Great Spirit* promote their growth. You cannot make the sun shine or rain fall. The storm is raging. When the storm is over, your soil will be conditioned just right. There will be sprouting. There's a process going on beneath the soil. Success is there.

You weren't created to fail. You were created to excel. Don't lose hope. Soon my friend, you'll be able to eat good fruit: fruit of mercy, fruit of healing, and the fruit of the Spirit. Get ready for your harvest. Keep pressing forward. Make room for heartache and disappointment to become issue of the past. Let negative thoughts be composted with waste. My friend, they'll be broken down to work in your favor.

The sun's behind the clouds. There's clear sky in the distance. You're coming into an abundance of sunshine. Believe in miracles.

Your light will shine bright. Your cup will run over. Your territory will be enlarged. You'll go beyond boundaries. You'll be kissed by wisdom and caressed by understanding. There will be a steady flow in traffic. My friend, you will arrive. There's pressure under the soil. Yes. Talent will sprout up with opportunity.

Salt of the earth, you've been downtrodden; count it all joy. There's a place prepared for you. Dine with the Divine. Take your seat at the table. Savor the moment: For you will dine with the King; you'll dance with the Prince; the Queen will anoint your head with precious oil. Be of good cheer my friend: you have a room prepared at the palace.

Chew on this, my friend, swallow it; its essential nutrient for the soul: there's pressure under the soil. The seeds you've sown are sprouting. Ready your baskets, a harvest like never before is on the way. You've survived the fall. You've survived the time when things crumbled at your feet. Your winter was colder than ever. The rains of spring seemed like they were never going to cease. Get ready! Those April showers will bring you May flowers: a summer full of sunshine draws near. Keep on pressing on. Find your reason to endure.

I'm reminded of the story of a man named Job who lived in a land of Uz. He was a wealthy man until his season changed. Everything crumbled at his feet: his livestock died, his servants died, his children died - all the same day. The blameless man continued to praise *The* Great Spirit.

Illness fell upon him. His wife encouraged him to give up: "Dost thou still retain thine integrity? Curse God, and die." Job refused. His friends questioned his faithfulness and accused him of doing evil. Job pressed on. Prior to his suffering the enemy conspired against him. It was never anything Job did wrong; instead, what he'd done right. The enemy believed God's favor upon Job was the reason he walked upright. God allowed Job to be tested. *The* Great Spirit knew how the story would end. God knew Job would press on.

Job passed the test. There was a whirlwind. The rain poured. After, the sun shined bright in Job's life once again. He was healed from illness, blessed with new children; his territory was enlarged. How did this happen? How did a man who appeared to have no hope; receive miracles and blessings? My friends, Job was humbled. He found a reason to keep on pressing on. He was blessed with double in his harvest.

You have friends and family who encourage you to give up. There are people in your life who accuse you due to lack of understanding. Don't be discouraged. Keep expecting your harvest. There's a rainbow of promise at the end of your storm. Look up my friend! Look for the sun behind the clouds.

The harvest marks the end of your growing season. What you sow in your conditioned soil has the potential to feed you for a lifetime. You only have to plant a perennial seed once to enjoy its fruit year after year. There's an old wise saying: "If you want a crop for a year, grow millet. If you want a crop for ten years, grow a tree. If you want a crop for one hundred years, grow men."

I cut the bottom off green onions I'd bought from the store. I planted them in a container. I didn't own land. I'd hoped it was possible to grow those onion scraps on my balcony. A few weeks later, I had onions.

My first harvest: a bunch of green onions, and three cherry tomatoes. It wasn't grand in variety; but, it was delicious. A week later, there were more green onions. They stood big and tall; as if to say: "You can try to cut me down; but, I'm not going anywhere, I will come back stronger than before." Maybe someone has tried to cut you down. You don't see the opportunity. You've experienced difficulty in circumstance. Your obstacles appear too big to overcome. Keep on pressing on. The sun will rise tomorrow. It's not over yet: there's still the harvest.

You may not feel equipped. You may not believe your dreams can come true. You may not know the right direction to drive in. My friend, keep going. Don't stop until you get there. Don't stop until you get to your destination. Don't stop watering those seeds you've sown in your conditioned soil: there's harvest in due season.

Get ready. Prepare for the harvest. Not some onions and a few tomatoes. Prepare for a harvest of more than enough. Prepare for abundance of favor, abundance of blessings, harvest of health, harvest of love, harvest of wisdom, knowledge, and understanding.

You will not see the same cloud in the sky forever; just as the speed of its movement, the same goes with your problems. They too vary in different colors, shapes, and sizes: but all move. They're temporary my friend. Don't focus on the clouds: focus on clear sky ahead. The sun will break through. This is the time of your harvest. Affliction will divide a man for the purpose of increase. It's best to be as the bush at this time - burnt but not consumed.

You may have heard, "Whatever you put into something is what you're going to get out of it." This is part of a truth. If you plant one seed in your garden of life it can grow and multiply; if it's the right kind of seed: planted at the right time of the year. If you place the same seed in an empty jar; without neither soil nor water, it will likely remain a seed.

My friend, be of good cheer: *The* Almighty who brought forth the grass, the herb yielding seed, and the fruit tree yielding fruit will increase you in favor. *The Great Spirit will ensure your harvest is good.* He wants you to arrive at your destination. He wants to heal you. He wants you to experience love, peace, and joy. Child of God, you're not destined to suffer for the rest of your life. It's not written that way. Plant the seeds and endure the time of waiting. Your season will change. Marvelous blessings will sprout up in your life. My friend, know the LORD will save you. You are His anointed. His right hand is at the ready.

Keep waiting, keep watching, and keep watering. Let your seeds for success take root. Yes. Let those roots take hold. Stand aside and witness a breakthrough. Something beautiful is springing up from the ground for you. It's pressing under the soil. Roots make way through dirt.

You doubt your abilities. You're saying to yourself: "I don't have a green thumb. I'm a drunk. I'm a prostitute. I'm not educated enough. I'm too old to *do this*," or, "I'm too young to *do that*." My friend, I've had my share of *what ifs*. I don't have a green thumb. My thumb is purple. There was a time my hands were amongst thorns. Through faith, I plant seeds.

Giver of good gifts, you're meant to plant your seeds. You "don't know how." It's ok. *The* Great Spirit's going to show you how. It's a part of the process. You need to be rooted before visible growth takes place. Do your part. Press against the soil. Demand your breakthrough. Sprout to your destiny.

Instead of telling yourself what you can't do; I dare you to start telling yourself what you can do. If you keep listening to people who tell you can't do what you've been called to do; and you believe them, you'll delay your growth.

Growing up, I was an active child. I was bullied until forced to fight back. The problem: I wouldn't stop. I was placed in a program for children with learning disabilities.

Junior year, I was advised by the high school counselor. I told her I wanted to take advance classes the following year. I wasn't surprised when she told me, "you can't." According to them I was a *"firecracker"*. No. I held my peace. I sat straight up in my chair; looked her in the eyes: *Who are you to tell me I can't do something; God tells me I can?* The counselor wept.

I was enrolled in advance classes. By the grace of God I made it through. How'd a young girl on a path to ruin change course? She believed *The* Great Spirit when He said: "You can." I pressed against the soil. I'm *gone* get my harvest.

My friend, you're destined for greatness. Your only limitation is to limit yourself. Moses was slow of speech but led the multitudes to freedom and thereafter. David was but a youth when he mastered a giant. You are a man who can do all things through *The* Great Spirit. Do not limit yourself. Believe all things are possible. My love, you'll sprout and grow into beauty from the ashes. One day, you'll provide the nutrients to keep another alive.

When you sow a seed, you increase your chances of an abundant harvest. David said, "He blesseth them also, so that they are multiplied greatly; and suffereth not their cattle to decrease." So shall it be for you my friend. Endure. Keep pressing on. Be like those green onions after they're cut down - come back stronger than before. Rise!

I've discovered for myself: what's impossible for man is possible for God. What doctors say can't be done, God says: "It's already done." What the enemy used to try to hurt you: *The* Great Spirit will turn it around to help you. When *so-called* friends turn their backs on you: God will place the right people on your path. When you want to learn; God will be your teacher. When you want to move; God will be your compass. When you want to grow; He says: "Plant these seeds. I'll give you increase."

The Great Spirit's provided you with seeds. All you have to do is plant, water, and wait. Some of us just have to plant the seeds. We're so close to our breakthrough; God says, "Step back, I'm about to make it rain." Your harvest could be today, in a few days, at the end of the week; maybe in seven years. No matter how long it takes, if you step out on faith and follow the instructions you're given, you'll experience a bountiful harvest.

Friends, the God I serve wants to help you. He's not concerned with what you look like. He's not concerned with where you come from. He's not concerned about what mama or daddy did. He's not concerned about where you're at right now. No. He knows where you're going.

Maybe you've already had a taste of your harvest. You already know of Gods favor. My friend, you don't know, "yet as you ought to know." This harvest will be one you've never seen before. You'll never forget again what *The* Great Spirit's done for you.

You're going to believe in miracles. You're going to trust and not doubt. You're going to testify of God's mercy saying, "In my weakness God remained strong. God made me whole. God touched me and I was healed. God opened the springs of His hands; gave me drink of living water. Yea, I lost my job; but, God promoted me. The enemy wanted to take my life; but, God saved me with His mighty right hand. Yea, they wanted to lock me up behind bars; but, God brought the truth to the light. Yea, I lost my mind; but, God helped me find it. They said I would never make it; but, the land yields its harvest; God our God, blesses..."

When I look in the mirror knowing where *The* Great Spirit's brought me from; the mess I was in He was able to get me out of; the sickness He healed: *"The land yields its harvest; God our God blesses..."*

My friends, labor for the sake of the harvest. Breakthrough! Sprout! Taste divine fruit - it's good.

There's a popular gospel song that says, "So good, I just can't tell it all." When I taste something good, sometimes, I can't do nothing but moan. I sound like an actor for Campbell Soup, "M'm! M'm! Good!" Folks around me cut their eyes and give me dirty looks; but, "I just can't help it." Let God overwhelm your taste buds. Take a bite of His divine fruit. It only takes one bite for the flavor of God to be in your mouth forevermore.

If you're discouraged, be encouraged. You're not defeated. You're supposed to breakthrough all that dirt and glory in the sun. Your destiny is meant to be beautiful. You're to bud in His favor. If good things aren't happening to you; if you can't get past the struggle; if all you do seems to fail: consider sowing another seed. Maybe you've sown a seed not acquired from God. If you plant a perennial seed from God, He promises your growth. Keep pressing against the soil my friend. Your harvest will be, "M'm! M'm! Good!"

I met a man who'd planted the wrong seed. He was growing in gang activity. He inspired me with his story. He was shot three times. A bullet entered his skull. He went blind. Not long after, he was diagnosed with cancer. At the time, everything seemed to be going wrong for Mr. Jackson; but, he refused to give up. The dirt kept falling back on him; but, he kept pressing. He had faith God could do the impossible.

He decided to sow another seed. He dedicated a song he'd written to *The* Great Spirit. I don't remember the words to the song; however, when he sung, the words cut straight through my flesh to enter my heart. He opened his eyes, "Sister, after I finished singing that song I began to see again."

My once blind brother shared fruit from his harvest. M'm! M'm! Good! Although he suffered from cancer at the time of our meeting; he wasn't concerned. He had the flavor of God in his mouth. He was expecting his harvest. He kept looking for the sun to rise. He knew if God could make a blind man see; God could make him cancer free. He gloried in the sun.

My friend, do you believe your sickness can be healed? Do you believe your circumstance will get better? Do you believe *The* Great Spirit can turn it around for you? Do you want to glory in the sun?

Have you sown the seeds of faith? Are you expecting your harvest? Or: Are you content believing a lie? Are you content believing you're a failure? Are you content believing you're not loved? Are you content believing you're addicted? Are you content believing you're defeated?

My friends, addictions do not last unless you want them to. You're not defeated until you give up. Don't throw in the towel. There's still the harvest. The sun will rise. It doesn't matter the situation. It doesn't matter how long you've struggled. Believe all things are possible for God. Keep pressing! He loves you. God fertilizes your soil. He feeds you. Absorb His goodness. My friend, rise above it all.

Don't worry about your enemies. God says: "I will prepare a table in their presence." Don't worry about that sickness. God says: "Come to me, I will give you rest." Don't worry about finances. God says: "I will supply all your needs." Don't worry about what people say. God says: "If you listen to me, you'll live in peace, untroubled by fear or harm." Don't worry about delay. God says: "I know the plans I've for you, they are plans for good and not disaster, to give you a future and a hope"

No worries. You're going to get your harvest. Your season will change. *The* Great Spirit's conditioning your soil. He'll fertilize you in favor. Take root. Grow. Emerge into your destiny. Your harvest will be bountiful. Your baskets will overflow. You'll have more than enough. Oh, "Taste and see that He is good."

Remember my friend: "It's always darkest before the dawn." It's dark out; but, there's a light in you. One flip of faith will allow you to see in darkness. One flip, allows you to keep the *monsters* of fear and hopelessness away. One flip of faith; and your enemies will run and hide. All things negative are afraid of the light in which you thrive.

Children hated me. It seemed like every time I went toward a child; they'd run the other way. One day, a little Caucasian boy did the opposite: he ran up to me out of nowhere. He grabbed hold. He hugged my legs as if he was hugging his favorite teddy bear. His family beckoned him to come. He wouldn't let go. He looked up at me. He smiled. His eyes welcomed a familiar face. Needless to say, he warmed my heart. I had turned the lights off; God sent a child to turn them back on. God sent a child to tell me, "I hear you." God sent a child to tell me, "I love you."

My neighbors have a two year old daughter named Vanessa. The day I met Vanessa, she was driving her car into a wall. Deja Vu! She ran to me with open arms. She wouldn't put them down until I picked her up. I spoke with her a while; then I was on my way. I thought to myself: *she thinks I'm someone she knows.*

A few days later, she and her grandmother were headed to Chuck E. Cheese's. I only saw the grandmother at first; but, before I could call the child by name, she was running to me with open arms.

What was happening? I was experiencing a harvest of God's love. David said, "Children are reward from God." God sent a child to tell me, "Remember." God sent a child to tell me, "I still hear you." God sent a child to tell me, "I still love you." God sent a child to tell me, "An even greater harvest draws near."

When I get discouraged; when I see only the impossible; when I'm tempted to shut the lights off and let the *monsters* have their way with me; I remember: *The* Great Spirit has a plan for my life.

My dear friend, may your harvest be bountiful. May your baskets overflow with grace, overflow with love, overflow with healing, overflow with advancement, overflow with victory, overflow with justice; yes, overflow with wisdom, knowledge, and understanding. Get ready for the harvest.

I understand you have a hard time believing in a God you can't see. Have you tried believing in the one you can see? You'll never be able to see Godly things; standing in ungodly places. You'll never be able to find what you don't seek. Only *The* Great Spirit knows your heart. What I'm about to tell you is organically out of love.

Little dove, travel back in time. Go back to when you stopped believing. Do you see it? Do you see someone's persuaded you to believe the way you do? Your turn my love. Do you see it? Do you see disappointment has caused you to believe the way you do? We've all lost something. Some loses hit harder than others. Don't blame God for this. It's not His fault. If you insist on blaming: blame Time. Time is the cause of change. My friend, do you see it? Do you see the greed of man has caused you to believe the way you do? False prophets, corrupt judges, and shady business men: not God.

Don't confuse God with man's idea of who He is. See Him for what He is. *The* Great Spirit's the precious air you breathe, the water you drink, the food you eat, the gravity that keeps you grounded; the sun that gives light and warmth. Yes. He's the wind that allows the world to be fruitful. He's every season to keep order. He's balance - *The* Architect - *The* creator of all things.

It's better to say you don't believe in a book, than to say you don't believe there's a God – it's a testament of ignorance. God is indeed all around you. My friend, not just around you: in you. Shush, Listen. Do you hear that? I can hear a heart beating. Your hate for Him will not change His love for you. That's why man can never be God - although at times we try.

Then there's you, I don't have to ask you do you see it. I know you do. You think it's cool to not believe. When asked you'll say, "I don't believe there's a God." When things begin to shake, rattle, and roll; you'll be the first one to fall on your knees. Those people you're trying to impress will abandon you. That money you think you've obtained on your own will be lost. Not a curse; but, my love, it's going to be your reality. This is when you'll know and never deny again, what is so. Step out of the box. Seek to find. Take those seeds out of your pocket and plant them. Flip on the switch of faith inside of you. Know beyond a shadow of doubt, "I AM is with you always!"

I declare by faith, these miraculous signs will accompany those who believe: you shall experience a harvest like never before; you shall arrive at your destiny; a child will be born; healing and restoration will take place; your relationships will get better; your enemies will run and hide. My friends, my fellow heirs, I declare; you shall overcome! Arise!

If you believe, it is done. God says, "If you abide in me, and my words abide in you, ask whatever you wish, and it will be done for you." However, remember my love, "Faith without works is dead."

Notice something about Vanessa: she kept her arms out stretched, and her hands opened wide until I picked her up. The little boy wouldn't let go; even though his parents beckoned for him. That's the way it should be for us. We should press until we get desired results.

It has been written: "Whosoever therefore shall humble himself as a little child, the same is great in His kingdom." We should hold on tighter to Him when *folks* try to pull us away. "Let the children come to me." He says, "And do not forbid them, for my kingdom belongs to such as these."

The Great Spirit calls to us. He beckons us to come. He gives us opportunity to read in His garden and run in His fields. He fills our baskets with good things. When the storm comes; He provides shelter in the palms of His hands. He sits us down at His table to consume His mercy. He gives us to drink of His grace.

The Great Spirit has more for you my love. What are you expecting? Are you expecting less? Are you questioning your worth? Are you not holding your hands up long enough? Are you letting go?

"By grace you've been saved through faith. And this is not your own doing; it's a gift from me." Plant the seeds. Keep pressing against the soil. You'll get your harvest. Believe God has more for you in spite of what it looks like. Believe you'll arrive. My friend, if you believe you have the favor of God - you have the favor of God.

I dare you to flip faith on: "God I know you're watching over me. I know you'll never leave me nor forsake me. I know your plan for my life's better than anything I could've put together myself. I know you love me. I know you'll deliver me from the hands of my enemies."

Lights of the world, keep your arms out stretched and your hands open wide. Grab hold to what's good. Hold on. Don't let go. Wait my friend. "Weeping may endure for a night, but joy cometh in the morning." Wait. Your harvest will be bountiful. So bountiful; you'll cry out on the rooftop, "the land yields its harvest; God our God, blesses..." It'll be so good - you won't be able to tell it all. The flavor of God will overwhelm your taste buds. My friends, it's going to be M'm! M'm! Good!

When I first heard instructions from God I struggled to follow them. Back then, I was quick to refuse. I was quick to tell God: *No.* I always had an excuse: *I can't tell them that - they're going to think I'm crazy - I'm too young - I'm not ready - They say according to you women aren't supposed to do that - I can't write like that; I'm in content mastery.*

He whispered, "Leave." I ignored Him. God kept whispering to me, "Leave." I just kept ignoring Him. He got louder and louder until He screamed. Yet, I still ignored. I wasn't ready to give up everything. I wasn't ready to leave my family and friends behind.

Suddenly, my season changed. Everything went wrong. I lost my job. I was moving from pillar to post, facing issues of academic delay – heartbreak - sickness. I found my enemies when looking for my friends. I cried out in frustration: *Are you still there God?* He responded with one word, "Leave."

I left home with the cloths on my back and an empty wallet in my pocket. My journey didn't last long. I failed my mission the same day. I returned home, crawled into bed, and that was that. Early morning, God screamed at me again, "LEAVE." I didn't hesitate. I didn't know where I was going; or what I was supposed to do, but my disobedience put the fear of God in me.

The cup of His favor began to overflow. Things lined up. He put the right people on my path. I didn't have to hunger. I didn't have to thirst. When it rained: not one hair on my head got wet. When it snowed: my feet remained warm. The flavor of God is good in my mouth - I can't get enough. It tasted so good I moaned. Folks cut their eyes at me, they gave me dirty looks; But, I just couldn't help it. I experienced a bountiful harvest. I could see for myself: "The land yields its harvest; God our God, blesses...."

If I kept the seed of obedience in my pocket; do you think I would've experienced a harvest? Or, if I'd placed my seed of faith in a jar without soil or water; do you think I would've rooted? What about the once blind man who planted the seed of talent? Or Job, when he planted the seed of endurance?

If God can make a blind man see; If He can make a cripple walk again; If He can make a barren woman conceive: He can get you that house you want. He'll get you approved for college. He can mediate between the two of you. *The* Great Spirit can promote you. He can help you overcome addiction. He can cause your pimp to run and hide. It takes one flip of faith. One flip: to turn the lights back on. One flip: to see your season change. One flip: for you to thrive. My friend, the sun is coming up. Glory!

Like a child, run to your Father with your arms out stretched and your hands open wide. Like a child, hold onto Him. Don't let go. No. Don't let go.

My friend, take the perennial seeds you've been given by God out of your pocket. Plant them. Take the perennial seeds you've been given by *The* Great Spirit out of that jar. Plant them. Give things time in your life to take root. Press against the soil. Arise! Oh Let the dirt fall to the side and sprout: "I'll cause the storm in your life to cease. I'll condition your soil. I'll bring forth my sun. I'll bring forth the honey bee. I'll supply and multiply your seed for sowing. You shall thrive in my favor. I will increase the harvest of your righteousness. Feed my sheep; and your gathering shall last until sowing time. You will thus eat your food to the full; and live securely in your land. You shall have the best of the best."

My friend, taste and see that He is good. M'm! M'm! Good! Folks may cut their eyes at you. They may give you dirty looks. No worries. The flavor of God is in your mouth. Tell them why He's good. Tell them why you can't help it. Make a joyful noise my friend. You've wept long enough. You're time of harvest is now.

24

Share your baskets with one another. Notice: David didn't say God just blessed him after the land yielded its harvest. No. He said, "The land yields its harvest; God our God, blesses us." What God has done for you, do for others. Share your sweet nectar. Pollinate your brothers and sisters. Show mercy because you've been shown mercy, and favor, because you have favor.

Friends, follow the instructions you're given by God. Trust Him. Plant the seeds and let *The* Great Spirit promote their growth. Wait. The sun will rise again. Wait. The sun will shine again. The earth remains seedtime and harvest. Givers of good gifts, make ready your baskets. Don't sleep on the harvest. For indeed: "The harvest is plentiful, but the workers are few." It's time to wake up now. Get up. Arise! It's almost time to gather the sheaves and begin the threshing. Harvest time is near.

Plant The Seeds

He who has health has hope,

and he who has hope has everything.

Ancient Proverb

Chapter Two:
Lather of God

I was visiting with some family when I was about five years old. They had a small house in the country. The back yard was foggy. Leaves covered the ground. That wasn't going to stop us. My cousin and I loved to race. We'd run as far as we could as fast as we could. I was winning the race; but, the fog was thick, I could no longer see where I was going. I didn't want to lose: so I kept running.

As I continued running towards the marked tree; my cousin stopped running. I didn't think to check on him; I just kept running towards that tree. I could hear him screaming something at me from a distance. A few seconds later, I tripped over a barbed wire. Fell face first into what I thought was a big puddle of mud.

When I made it back to the house: I was laughed at, cursed out, and avoided. I didn't understand why I was being treating that way. I tried not to let it bother me. After all, it was only mud. No. I'd fallen into a cesspool. After realizing how dirty I was, I began to cry. My aunt prepared a bath for me in the family room. She didn't laugh. She didn't curse at me. She didn't avoid me. She did what she knew had to be done. She cleaned me up.

It was hard work, but somebody had to do it. First, she bathed me with soap. Then, she bathed me again with fresh tomatoes and ketchup. After she rinsed and dried me off; she poured a whole bottle of baby powder on me. She didn't stop there. She provided me with fresh clothing. She dressed me up and combed my hair. When she was all done with me; not only was I clean: I looked good, and I smelt good.

In the same way, all God has to do is put His hands on you - you'll have a fresh start. One touch of His mercy can wash away all those years of being covered in filth. You can be labeled a *good for nothing drunk,* known for being passed out on the sidewalk resting in vomit; spending each day feeling guilty about something that happened some fifty years past. You don't have to cry. A mumble is all it would take for God to clean you up. One mumble to God can take your face out of that mess.

Suddenly, you're walking fresh and smelling good. Suddenly, folks don't recognize you. Suddenly, you look in the mirror and you're amazed: you didn't know you could look so good.

What happened? You mumbled and God put His hands on you. He washed you clean from guilt. He lathered you with salvation. He gave you a clean new heart. Yes. *The* Great Spirit has given you a fresh start. He cured you of liver disease. He restored and reunited you with your family. You looked so good, you didn't want to hide.

That's what happens when God gets His hands on you: God cleans you up. Your situation stinks badly. People run away from you. No worries. When *The* Great Spirit cleans you up; covers you from head to toe with His scent - the people who ran from you will run to you.

You feel hopeless. The fog's thick. You can't see your way through. You feel ugly inside and out. You feel it's too late to get up from vomit. The voices in your head are telling you: "You'll never be able to find another job. It's your fault you were abused. You'll never be able to overcome addiction. You're worthless. Look what God did to you. He doesn't love you." My friend, you feel like every negative thing people say to you about you is truth. But God's saying: "Get up, follow me, I've prepared a bath for you."

God protects you when you follow Him. He removes harmful things from your path. He opens doors and holds them open. When the enemy tries to close a door in your face; *The* Great Spirit takes the door off the hinges. Walk into your destiny. He'll show you how to get around road blocks. My friend, overcome. Trust *The* Great Spirit. Believe He can do what He says He can do - wash you clean. If you mumble to God like King David and say, "Create in me a clean heart, O God; and renew a right spirit within me," you'd get a fresh start.

I speak life and not death. I speak of hope and the light; in truth, that you may overcome your struggles.

Many of you are covered in filth. Suffer it to be so now. The loofah of God's salvation is lathered. With the touch of His hands your bath is warmed. He removed old things: to cover you in newness. He says, "Come now, step into your future. I shall do wonderful things for you. Though your sins be as scarlet, they shall be as white as snow; though they be red like crimson, they shall be as wool."

It doesn't matter what kind of mess you're in. It doesn't matter how strong the scent. One toe into God's grace gets you closer to your fresh start. Things in your life headed to destruction will turn around to find the path of good. You'll be able to see you again. You'll remember who you are. Your enemies will be hushed by how bright you shine. Yes. Those negative voices in your head will disappear.

My brother and sisters, there's a bath prepared for you in the presence of *The* Great Spirit. Get up from your mess. Go to Him. He'll wash you white as snow. He'll cloth you in your right minds. You don't have to feel ashamed. God's not going to laugh at you. He's not going to curse you out. He's not avoiding you. No. He knows what needs to be done - He will do it with ease.

Hope To A Friend ⬩ Sunrise

He says, "I know the plans I've for you...they are plans for good and not disaster, to give you a future and a hope." Yes. You'll live to see the sun rise again. My love, if you believe, in faith, "It's done." You are clean!

My friend, you have the favor of God upon your life. You're cured and made whole. Your season has changed. Addictions and bad habits have no weight on you. *The* Great Spirit has tied the ribbon. Your scent is pleasing to my nostrils. You are beautiful. Look in the mirror and glory at the work of God.

The bath is your salvation. It's not of this world. No man gives it, not by words, nor by hands; no man can take it away, not by force, or by curse; it's a gift from God. You mumble and it thunders in the clouds. Folks laugh at you - they don't understand. They poke at you - they think you're weak. God says, "I hear only the words of your heart. I am your strength. Lean on me. I will hold you up."

This is God promising to take you where you need to go. He's not saying: "You need to be able to stand straight." He's saying, "Cry out as a daughter in need to a mother. Mumble as a son in need to a father.

I'll pick you up from foul and dung. I'll wash you white as snow. I'll place you on the mountain top."

My friend, the bottle is not your refuge. Drugs will not enlighten you. Sex will not fill the void. Running away doesn't mean you'll get away. Giving up doesn't mean you'll succeed.

God knows what needs to be done. Let Him be your refuge. Let Him fill your void. Listen as He enlightens you of the plan. Run into His arms. For it has been written: "The eternal God is thy refuge, and underneath are the everlasting arms: and He shall thrust out the enemy from before thee..." Oh my dear friends, "Behold, the LORD'S hand is not shortened, that it cannot save; neither His ear heavy, that it cannot hear..." No. God will wash away the filth and remove the gunk from your eyes. You will see again.

When God puts His hands on you, your new attitude should be: "God, thank you for cleansing me. Thank you for a clean new heart. Thank you for renewing a right spirit within me. Thank you for clothing me in my right mind. Thank you for perfuming me in favor. Thank you for making me look good. Thank you for making me walk straight. Thank you for making me talk straight. Thank you for healing me of cancer. Thank you for keeping my child safe. Thank you for a job. Thank you for salvation. Thank you for deliverance. Thank you for helping me breakthrough. God, I know you have a better plan for my life. God, I'm going to trust you. God, I'm going to walk by faith and not by sight. God, I'm going to believe you can do all things impossible. God, I'm going to believe in your power. The land yields its harvest; God our God, blesses... M'm! M'm! Good!" Yes. Be grateful.

Smell yourself. The old you is washed away. The crud that held you down is not there anymore. You don't reek of addiction. There's nothing holding you back. The sky is your limit. God's your ultimate goal.

You should no longer say what you *can't* do. You should no longer say what's *too late* to do. No. God's given you a fresh start. If you'll make some moves; others will get a whiff of God's favor on you. The smell of God is intoxicating. My friend, people will follow you. Doors will open. Things will line up. Before, they pushed you out; now, they will beg you in. Before, they stepped on you; now, you're out of their reach. Before, you were lying in vomit; now, how bright you shine.

One of my good friends struggled with drug abuse. When I met him, we were both going from shelter to shelter for hot meals and rest. I noticed him on the work van. No, it wasn't his light-skinned handsome appearance - or his welcoming eyes. He didn't look like the others. He didn't talk like the others. He didn't even smell like the others. His shoes were clean and shiny.

One day he went missing. I looked for him. I couldn't find him. He'd checked himself into a rehab program. I was surprised. Yes. I was amazed when he shared his story with me. I couldn't believe it. I couldn't believe the man who'd encouraged me on my journey was as dirty as he said he was.

Two days out of the week I'd get a chance to see my friend after worship. He started cutting hair for other homeless men. He was quite the barber. This was his ministry he explained. I'd sit there listening to him encourage young men to do the right thing. I'd sit there watching my once dirty brother shine. I could see the sun rising.

What happened? My friend Aaron mumbled, and it thundered in the clouds. God prepared a bath for him. Aaron decided to test the water first: he put his toes in - that's why his shoes shined. When he discovered the water was just right; like a child, he humbled himself and dove in. Now, he's clean from head to toe. Others can see him shine. Others smell the scent of God on him and follow. Yes. *The* Great Spirit gave my friend Aaron a fresh start.

Joseph was stripped of his robe and thrown into a pit by his brothers. They laughed when he cried for help. They held their nose to his scent. They didn't like the smell of obedience. No. They enjoyed the fragrance of vengeance, and the mustiness of pride. They sold Joseph into slavery for twenty pieces of silver.

While in slavery: Joseph was mocked, beaten, and mistreated. But there was something different about this young man. People began to get a whiff of something. Yes. They began to smell the scent of God on him.

Joseph looked so good; he was lusted after by another man's wife. When she was refused; she falsely accused him. Joseph was thrown into prison. Nevertheless, God had a plan. He put the right people in prison with the young man. Joseph began to shine.

He interpreted a dream for a cupbearer and a baker. The interpretation was good for the cupbearer; he returned to Pharaoh's favor. The baker was put to death.

My friend, no matter the circumstance, *The* Great Spirit anointed Joseph to overcome. It's as if God was saying to Joseph: "Your praise continues to pierce the clouds. I've cleansed you. I've washed you white as snow. I'll let no man bring you harm. You look too good to be here. I shall sit you on high. Even your enemies shall glory at my good work." God kept His promise to Joseph. The shepherd was made governor over all of Egypt. His enemies were made his footstool; but, Joseph didn't rest his feet upon them.

God planned Joseph's success from the time of his youth. *The* Great Spirit took the shepherd boy and cleaned him up. He didn't just make him look good. He didn't just make him smell good. No. God gave Joseph a bountiful harvest. The same people that use to laugh at him; the same people that pushed him down; the same people that meant to kill him: had to go before his face in want. God cleaned Joseph up so well; his own brothers couldn't recognize him.

If you mumble to God, He promises to clean you up. He promises to give you a fresh start. Like Joseph, you'll rise to bless your enemies. Step into the tub of righteousness. Oh be made clean. Lather in God's salvation. Yes. Hold to His truth in love.

Some people in your life may close their nose to the scent of God on you. Maybe they try to put you back in foul and dung. They can't see you've changed. They say, "You'll never be nothing but a drunk. You'll never be nothing but a thief. You'll never be nothing but a bastard. You'll never be nothing but a whore. I hate you. You think you're better than me? You're good-for-nothing and nobody."

Do not be discouraged. Step out of the way. God roars in the heavens: "What I've cleansed do not call common."

In junior college, I wasn't liked by the other girls; especially in my criminal justice class. They'd point and laugh at me. I'd hear them say, "Look what she got on. She looks a hot mess. I hate her." Yes. I studied long to cipher what I did to offend them. The problem didn't make sense to me. I smiled and greeted them well. No. Those girls didn't like the scent of God on me.

Lather of God

Around the same time, I received a phone call from my then boyfriend's mother, "Do you know anything about Allen's window being busted out of his car?" I answered her question truthfully with respect: *No ma'am. You don't think I did it do you?* The preacher's wife didn't hesitate to speak, "YES I DO...You crazy bitch! You crazy whore!" I cried.

I never gave her a reason to treat me like that. I'd looked up to her since I was a child. She judged me based on shortcomings. She saw what she wanted to see in my past. She saw a child being raised by one parent. Amazing, how a person could see so much; yet still be blind. I sparkled from head to toe in love. No. She didn't like the scent of God on me. She was wearing imitation God - I wear Name-brand.

Move. God's given you a fresh start. You have a choice: act in the role of your past, or, embrace the path of your future. My friend, you've been saved from all uncleanliness - sprinkled with pure water - cleansed of iniquity. Oh my love, "Let us draw near with a true heart in full assurance of faith, having our hearts sprinkled from an evil conscience, and our bodies washed with pure water."

Stop worrying about what *folks* think about you. Start listening to what God *says* to you. My friend, get up. Walk in newness. God didn't just clean you up. No. He polished you. You sparkle. The ribbon of righteousness glows on the top of your head. Walk into the dark room carrying the sun. Call unto God; He'll show you great and mighty things. Be showered in goodness, fragranced in mercy, and clothed in His grace.

Remember, "Ye are of God, little children, and have overcome them: because greater is He that is in you, than he that is in the world." The mouth of those who cast the stone shall be filled with the dirt of the grave. Wish no harm to come to others, or it shall come to you. Instead, pray *The* Great Spirit prepares their bath. Yes. Pray *The* Great Spirit Cleanses them of their foul and dung.

God's going to do exceedingly, abundantly, above, and beyond for you. He's going to sprinkle you with His fragrance. One drop is all it'll take. One drop of God's scent will give you a fresh start. You can have a family. You can go back to school. You can start that business. You can write that book. What takes years for others;

40

you'll do in a matter of months. The sky's the limit for you my love; but *The* Great Spirit's your ultimate goal.

There's a story about a man named Saul. This man went around persecuting anyone who followed *The* Great Spirit. One day, Saul fell to the ground. He got dirty. God prepared a bath for him. In an instant, Saul was restored. In an instant, Saul was clean.

What happened? God washed Saul white as snow: to give Paul a fresh start. Notice: God didn't curse, He didn't laugh, He didn't avoid. No. He did what needed to be done. *The* Great Spirit prepared the bath. He wasn't concerned with what Paul looked like. He wasn't concerned with where Paul came from. No. He could see where Paul was going. God put His hands on Saul. God lathered Saul with salvation. He provided him with a clean heart. Paul looked so good; he didn't want to hide.

That's what happens when you're chosen by God. He cleans you up. He prepares the way. He'll put you in position to be seen; that others may glory at His good work.

Maybe you were a liar. Maybe you were a thief. Maybe you were a bully. Maybe you were a cheater.

Maybe you were a drunk. Maybe you were a prostitute. Maybe you were on drugs. Maybe you were mentally ill. You're not anymore.

No. You've been washed clean by the hands of God. You've been sanctified. You've been justified. Now, you are: "Light of the world, salt of the earth, branch of the true vine; lover and friend; fellow heir, saint, giver of good gifts; a new creature, a chosen instrument, deserving, and redeemed."

People might not like the scent of God on you. They may close their nose to your presence. Keep right on doing what you're supposed to be doing: shine! Your enemies will try to throw mud on you. They'll try to stand in the way of your blessings. Don't worry about them. Keep right on doing what you are supposed to be doing: shine! Can't nothing or no one stop you from getting what *The* Great Spirit has for you. No foul smell - not above, nor below; can cover the scent of God on you. There's no amount of earth - not now, nor ever, that could make unclean; what *The* Great Spirit has cleansed.

Friends, mumble the words. Run to Him with arms out stretched and hands opened wide. God will clean you up. He saves whom He chooses. He knows who you are. He knows all about what you've done. Learn from it. He says, "Come to me, I will cleanse you from all unrighteousness." Get up and run to your Father.

I declare by faith, you no longer have to think: "Nothing will ever get better for me. There's nothing I can do to improve my situation." No. You no longer have to feel worthless, guilty, or ashamed. You no longer have to make yourself sick with unforgiveness. You no longer have to run and hide. You no longer have to lose sleep worrying. You no longer have to feel weak. You no longer have to be angry. You no longer have to walk around in foul and dung. No. My friend, be of good cheer. You are clean!

Maybe you're homeless. You're losing hope your finances will get better. When you get up you fall back down. Mumble to God; He'll pick you up. Lean on *The Great Spirit*; He'll carry you where you need to go. Stop wearing bootleg imitation God. His name-brand fragrance doesn't cost you anything - it's free to all.

Get up my friend! Go into the house and say to your Father: "Be gracious to me, O God, according to your loving kindness; according to the greatness of your compassion blot out my transgressions. Wash me thoroughly from my iniquity and cleanse me..."

The Great Spirit's Preparing A Bath For You.

Chapter Three:
Constant Flow

Jogging up a hill not long ago, I noticed a constant flow of water streaming down both sides of the road. I couldn't see where the water was coming from; it just kept flowing my way. As I struggled up the hill, 198 pounds, two and a half miles of a five mile run; I thought I was going to pass out. I was tired, hot, and dirty. I wanted to stop. I wanted to give up; but *The Great Spirit* gave me strength.

Lights of the world, I encourage you to keep moving forward. Maybe you've failed in the past. The task was too hard. It's taking too long to get there. Obstacles block the path ahead. It looks like you're never going to reach your destination. It looks like you're on the path to failure. My friend, be of good cheer: as the water streams from the top of the hills; God's flow of blessings are constant for you.

Yes. Your blessings are flowing like a stream from the mountain top. Your promotion is in the stream. Your healing is in the stream. Your confidence is in the stream. Your victory is in the stream. Your marriage is in the stream. Your justice is in the stream. Your restoration is in the stream. Keep moving forward. Meet your blessings halfway. You'll get a constant flow. No. Not a drop of God's grace; not a muddy puddle: a constant flowing stream of His goodness, favor, love, grace, and His mercy.

I put the ministry on hold to join the United States Navy. I was scheduled to leave home the following year. That wasn't good enough for me; I needed to get away from a relationship gone wrong. I sacrificed my original rating. I entered the service as an undesignated seaman.

In boot camp, I was considered one of the top of my division. I had high hopes for my future. I was recruited to work in personnel less than two weeks on my duty ship. Six months later, I advanced to a petty officer of religious programs. At that point, it looked like my dreams were going to come true with ease. However, I felt a weight upon me. I became forgetful. I couldn't think clear. The enemy said to me, "Jump."

No. I knew better than that. I decided to seek help. A few weeks later, I had a breakdown. That was the beginning to the end of my military career. I was discharged with a general under honorable for malingering; despite evidence of a medical condition. I wasn't even paid my last few weeks in service.

I lost hope. I couldn't pray. I wouldn't eat. Sleep was far from me. I was embarrassed - ashamed. Yes. I felt lost, alone, and betrayed. I could for the first time see the world with eyes of hate. My heart was covered with fat and my lips with bitterness. The faster I'd try to get up; the harder I'd fall back down.

Everything went wrong. I finally gave up. I tried to commit suicide. I'd lock myself up in closets to try to get away from it all. I'd sit in darkness; hoping, it would all just go away. Friends and family couldn't understand.

One day my neighbor, "Mr. Dean," learned my circumstance. He was a retired lawyer. I remember he spoke to me with a stern voice; encouraging me not to be so stubborn. I wanted nothing to do with any of it. I was hurt enough. In my mind, I knew how it was going to turn out. But ole "Mr. Dean," he would hear none of that. He took me to get help.

Shortly after, I received a deposit for $25,000 dollars along with a letter in the mail. The letter explained: there was more. That's a constant flow. Yes. I had to lose to gain. Although it didn't fix all my problems; it assured me, God still had His hands on me. It assured me; He's my lawyer: the one to bring me justice. It assured me; He's the author and the finisher of my *fate*. I can trust Him.

My friend, your life may seem dry; you've experienced drought; you feel hurt – helpless - lonely. Maybe the pressure at work is overwhelming. The strain to pay a bill is exhausting. You can't seem to find your way out of a situation. All the facts are telling you your life is over. My friend, be of good cheer: I'm here to tell you, God's poured out a stream of blessings for you. He's saying today: "Keep moving forward. I'm sending you the tools to mend broken hearts. I'm sending you a companion. I'm sending you favor for advancement. I'm sending you a way out." It's in the stream.

The word *constant*, can be defined as "Something that occurs continuously over a period of time" or, "A situation/state of affairs that doesn't change." My friend, God has sent you a lasting blessing. I wouldn't even bother to check for an expiration date. It will not spoil; nor sour in the stomach. It's for good health and prosperity: "to give you a future and a hope."

No. You're not a failure. If what you do isn't in line with what you're supposed to be doing; you will not succeed at it. Yes. You'll fail. Not as a person. You'll fail that assignment - because it's the wrong assignment. When you're walking according to your purpose; there's not a demon or devil in "hell" that can stop you. There's not a man on earth that can take it from you - it's your birthright. Your destiny belongs to you. No one can live your life for you.

My friend, your life's not over. The end of something is a new begging in disguise. Keep moving forward. You're approaching a constant flow. I declare, you won't have to worry. You won't have to be afraid. No.

The salted tears you cry in sadness will turn sweet with joy.

If you're tired; drink living water. It strengthens the bones and straightens the back. If you're hot; find shade in His shadow. *The* Great Spirit will lead the way - He'll provide cool breeze. If you're dirty; go into the house. God will clean you up.

I know the journey's been ruff. The heart's been beaten and bruised. The hills are steep. Don't let it stop you. God can make the ruff smooth. He can heal your heart. He can make the bruises disappear without a trace – if you let Him. Oh my dear friend, let Him give you the strength to climb that high mountain.

You may reason within yourselves saying, "Where is God? He wasn't there when I was evicted. He didn't stop my divorce. He didn't keep my child safe." I've learned God's always present. We just look for Him in the wrong direction. Sometimes, we look down when He's up; we look left when He's right; or, we look behind when He's ahead: smoothing, healing, opening doors, and pouring out streams.

Yes. God's the high point in which the rivers and the streams flow. When you see the stream; know you're closer to *The* Great Spirit. This is when your attitude should be: "I'm not gone give up. I'm going to try harder. I'm won't stop. I'm too close to quit. I know what I need's in the stream. I'm expecting a miracle. I'm expecting a breakthrough. I'm expecting a harvest. I'm expecting advancement. I'm expecting the fruits of the Spirit. I'm expecting my child to come home. I'm expecting my bills to be paid. I'm expecting healing. I'm expecting a fresh start. I'm expecting constant flow." My friend, whatever you're expecting in faith; it's in the stream.

Your constant flow of blessings from the most high is making its way down to you. It doesn't matter your location. God says, "I will open rivers in high places, and fountains in the midst of the valleys: I will make the wilderness a pool of water, and the dry land springs."

Your movement forward in spite of circumstance is equivalent to being steadfast. Don't stop. Keep going. You're going to get your constant flow. "God is not a man that He should lie;" He's going to do what He said. He's made a promise to you. Be of good cheer my friend; He'll make good on His promise.

The enemy's thrown debris to block the flow of your stream. No worries. God commands your blessing to flow around, over, and under. His stream doesn't stop. It will never dry up. It's always constant. It's flowing in your direction. You don't have to look for it. You don't even have to know it exists. Grace will find you. My friend, "Praise God from whom all blessings flow..."

Constant flow will cut a new path into the earth. Overtime, it will change the land and make the way. Rocks, pebbles, and soil; will be carried downstream to form new land. Nevertheless, it will continue to make deposits in your life.

Yes. Everything the enemy's thrown on your path is forming new land area. *Talk about stomping a snake on the head.* No. We'll walk all over it. What the enemy thought was going to stop you; God is using it to bless you. *The* Great Spirit's using it to enlarge your territory.

Go ahead. Walk all over depression. Walk all over addiction. Walk all over heartache. Walk all over fear. Walk all over guilt. Yes. Walk all over unforgiveness. Walk all over insecurities. Walk all over shame. Go ahead. Walk all over that eviction notice. Walk all over that warrant for your arrest. Yes. You'll walk all over disease; and it will not, because cannot harm you saint. Remember this little dove.

The stream is not selfish. There's something in there with your name on it. *The* Great Spirit released it from the top of the hill before you were born. My friend, your steps are ordered. God's placed within you a door of destiny; He's given you the keys to unlock it.

You want to start a business; God says, "I'm sending you the plan: it's in the stream." You want to write that book; God says, "I'm sending you the outline: it's in the stream." You want to invent something; God says, "The blueprints are on the way: it's in the stream." Yes. Wisdom, knowledge, and understanding are in the stream; with these three you're destined for greatness.

Keep moving forward in spite of what things look like. Meet your blessings halfway. *The* Great Spirit will provide you with everything you need to become. It's time to start running towards the source. It's time to walk all over the debris of the enemy. It's time to receive a constant flow from *The* Great Spirit. He's making you a blessing. It's the season my friend. Oh how the Lord showers down blessings upon the anointed – those whom are called according to His purpose.

My friend, you may not be able to see the finishing line; but I assure you, the race is already won. Be of good cheer. Keep moving to receive your reward. You may see the narrow part of the river, but you're headed towards the life spring. You may think, "This is all God has for me." No my love; there's more: it's in the stream. If I tell you the magnitude you won't believe me. It's impossible for man. God says, "I am working a work this day, which you will not believe, though it be told to you." Where is your faith? Find it.

Nobody can stake a claim in what *The* Great Spirit has for you. You don't have to be in competition for it; it belongs to you. He's not going to take it back. He poured it out already. No other key can unlock the door with your name on it - except the one you're carrying within your person; no other key can lock it - except the one in your hand.

God's done wonderful things for you my friend. You have no idea. You haven't reached that part of the stream yet. You've yet to splash in His exceeding favor. Your blessings are constant my love. No matter what debris the enemy throws on your path to try to stop you; through God's strength, by His grace and mercy - run through and leap over. That debris is forming new land masses for you to walk all over. God our GOD is enlarging your territory. Look up my friend. See the light shining bright. See deliverance. See healing. See joy. Oh my love; see hope. Hallelujah! Your greater is coming. Don't be afraid little dove. Everything's going to be alright. Don't quit. Don't stop. Don't give up. Look to the hills from which cometh your help. Your help comes from the LORD who made heaven and earth.

Salt of the earth, I encourage you to keep going in the direction of righteousness. Keep moving towards a love that never fails. Keep running from darkness into the light. Keep your feet covered in faith. Keep waiting for the sun to rise again. God says, "I will provide you with constant flow." It's going to be a constant flow of His goodness; a constant flow of His favor; a constant flow of His grace. It will not be a spot here and there. It won't be murky. It's going to be clear: *The* Great Spirit's blessing you - over and over again.

Your mother will not be able to explain it. Your father will not be able to explain it. Your sister will not be able to explain it. Your brother will not be able to explain it. No. Your friends and lovers will not be able to explain it. You will know - you just won't be able to tell it all. Your mouth will be too busy with praise. M'm! M'm! Good! "The land yields its harvest; God our God, blesses..."

When we speak life into a situation, it gives birth to good outcome. When we speak death, our dreams are consumed by the issues of this world. That's why I speak life and not death; victory and not defeat. You're neither dead nor defeated. Even if you've already stopped moving, you can start again.

My friend, God knows what you have. He knows what you need. He doesn't ask you to be superhuman. Do the best you can do. Go as far as you can possibly go. Trust Him enough to faint into His arms; knowing, He'll catch you. It has been written: "Even youths will become weak and tired, and young men will fall in exhaustion. But those who trust in God will find new strength. They shall mount up with wings like eagles;

they shall run, and not be weary; and they shall walk, and not faint."

You don't have to run. You can walk to your destination. Some of us are going to fly, some of us are going to be carried; but we're all moving forward towards the source. We're going to be tempted to turn back. Our faith will be tried and tested. Someone, or something, will drag on your coattail - trying to slow progress. My friend, take off the coat and keep moving. Meet your blessings halfway. God has provided you with constant flow.

Is that job slowing you down? Take off the coat. Is that relationship causing frequent stops? Take off the coat. Are your friends pulling you to the ground? Take off the coat. Never let anything hinder your steps towards the source. You have an assignment. You're not like everyone else. You're different. Yes. You're special. Yes. You're anointed. Yes. You've been chosen. You can't do what they do. Friends, you don't have to journey alone; others are traveling in the same direction with lanterns.

Keep moving in faith. Don't make up excuses to stop. It will slow progress. It may seem like a lot. It may seem like forever. My friend, time is not an issue. If I had a stamp for every journey *The* Great Spirit has taken me on, each one would say with bold letters: WORTH IT!

Prophet Elijah for a time failed to trust in God. He was tempted to quit. He was tempted to give up. He begged God that he should die. But God had plans for Elisha. They were to give him a future and a hope.

Like Elijah, you may be tempted to run scared. You may stop and beg to die under a tree. You may feel like a failure. People may talk about you. People may call you names. They may criticize your work. They may threaten your life. Yes. You will be misunderstood. But God knows the plans He has for you.

He's going to wake you up if He finds you sleeping. He's going to send His messengers to feed you: that you may have strength to go on. He's going to take care of not some; but my friend, all of your needs. I don't know who you are. I don't know what you look like. But I do know this: there's a constant flow coming your way.

You may have quit on God, but He hasn't quit on you. He's not going to let you die void. He stands at the top of the hill looking down on your progress.

He's watching your every move towards Him like the virtuous women awaiting her families return.

I'm not encouraging you to be a busybody. I'm encouraging you to plant the seeds and grow in faith. I'm encouraging you to follow the directions given by God. I'm encouraging you to make progress; even if it takes a hundred years to gather the materials needed. My friend, no worries: He has His hands on you.

You're destined to lead. You're destined to be the head and not the tail. You're destined to be the lender and not the borrower. Get up and move!

Friends, wanting something usually come with a price; but, in wanting nothing, you have everything you need. Do you want more of *The* Great Spirit? If so, prepare your hearts and follow Him. Follow Him wherever He may lead. He's not going to make you go back to what you've come from. It's your choice to return. Have an attitude like Paul and say: "Forgetting those things which are behind, and reaching forward to those things which are ahead, I press toward the goal for the prize..." My friend, there's no prize greater than the one God gives.

Hope To A Friend ⁕ Sunrise

Don't be discouraged. Be encouraged and strengthened in faith. If you shall for a moment taste of dust; spit it out, and drink from the constant flowing stream of God's mercy. My friend, wash the salt from your face and go. Hear the whispers and moans of the wind. Be replenished: "Come. You can do it! You can make it! I am here."

Don't be troubled within for good doing. It's through love that God is pleased. If you faint; fall into His arms and He'll carry you the rest of the way. If you fall to the ground; call for Him, He'll pick you up. Yes. He will dust you off. Do not fear. Don't be dismayed: For *I Am* is with you. Yes. *The* Great Spirit says, "For I am thy God: I will strengthen thee; yea, I will help thee; yea, I will uphold thee with the right hand of my righteousness." My friend, keep going!

Hold On A Little While Longer

Chapter Four:
Hot Pot

My friend, let go of that hot pot; it's burning your hands. If someone has hurt you, and you're holding onto that pain, anger, or fear; you're locking yourself in a cage; holding yourself back from freedom; holding yourself back from experiencing joy; holding yourself back from what The Great Spirit has for you.

When you have unforgiveness in your heart; to move forward, you have to let go of those hard feelings held against someone who's done you wrong. It doesn't matter what they did or how they did it. It doesn't matter who they are or why they felt the need. My friend, pick up the key to the cage. Set yourself free. Tend to your wounds before you're scarred for life.

Unforgiveness is a poison. It doesn't just harm you, it harms others around you. Not only can it make relationships go bad; it can also make you sick mentally, physically, and spiritually. When you come to a point where you can say: "I'm going to love in spite of. I'm going to choose not to be cold. I'm going to choose not to be bitter. I'm going to choose to trust in God:" you're putting your troubles in the pot. My Friend, God will turn up the heat on that pot. No worries. He'll provide you with a cool handle.

I know it's hard to forgive someone who molested and raped you. To forgive someone who's beaten your flesh to the white meat. To forgive someone who's cheated and manipulated you. To forgive someone who's taken a life of a loved one. It looks like you'll never be the same. My friend, you won't be. If you forgive you'll be better than before. Overcome. You don't have to keep reliving that experience over and over again. My friend, let it go. Don't do it for them: do it for you.

Don't let them have control of your life. They've taken so much from you already. Enough is enough. Get up. Wipe your eyes. My friend, take your life back.

It's going to take a while for you to heal; however, you can heal. You're not hurting them. They're sleeping good at night. You're hurting you. Take the knife out of that wound. Allow yourself to heal from this.

You can't keep this. Let it go. Don't think this is all life has to offer you. No my love. There's balance and order. If your start was ugly; it's because you're destined to have a beautiful finish. You're not being cheated. You're not being punished. You're being set up for good.

Yes. You were wronged. Yes. You were betrayed. Yes. You feel pain. You're numb: constantly living in fear - unable to trust people. My friend, if you take the knife out of that wound; you can heal from this. If you start making steps towards the life you want; you'll have a new beginning. It takes one step forward to begin again my friend. You can start now. Start by saying, _____I forgive you. You don't have to tell them - tell you. Forgive for you. I know many of you feel at fault. This is not your fault. Forgive you for blaming you. Do whatever you can to get over this my love. Move forward. The enemy's desperate. He knows what's ahead for you. He's scared of you. Don't let him win.

My friend, throw it in the pot. Throw Guilt in the pot. Throw fear in the pot. Throw shame in the pot. Don't concern yourself with foolish matters. It's a trick. A trick you don't see coming: lessen you pay close attention. You have to stay watchful. The enemy has no limitation in movement. He comes from all directions. He doesn't care about tearing a family apart. He does this for sport. He'll help you tear up the pieces; then, leave you alone with the mess. He loves to see the ones you love easily turn their backs on you.

Remember who the real enemy is. When you don't get worked up by his antics; he'll move on to the next, then the next - then the next. My friend, none of it will work. We're at constant war. Make no mistake about it. You have an enemy. Some call him the Devil. Me, I call him *Greed* - because he thrives off of lack. He loves guilt. To keep you in place is his favorite thing to do. He says: "Yeah right, you, you, the man that use to sell drugs for a living, a preacher? Ha. You can't do that. No one's going to listen to you. Ha. And you drink, you smoke, you party, you fornicate; you're a hypocrite, a whore, a drunk: you'll never be anything more than that." He says, "Look what they did to you.

You gonna to let them get away with that?" He says, "Take it. You got to have it: you need more." He says, "Do it. Nobody's ever going to know." Then, he'll use whatever he tempted you to do against you. He'll say, "It's your fault".

My friend, the enemy is not called a snake for no reason. A viper in the grass is real. It will bite you if you get close enough to let it. Don't let that snake bite you. No. Don't let him keep you down there; crawling on the ground eating dust with him. No. Get up.

My friend, you may not have had a perfect childhood. The people raising you may not have done a good job. Maybe you've been laid off from work. Use this to get you there. Learn from those bad parents how to be a good parent. See this layoff as opportunity for promotion: apply for a better job. Don't settle. You're worth so much more than you're giving yourself. Stop making up excuses to be bitter. Stop making excuses. Take the knife out of that wound and allow yourself to heal from this. Forgive. Too many people go through life mad at the world. Too many people place blame and point fingers: thinking somebody owes them something. No. They don't owe you anything. You owe yourself everything. You're your responsibility. Eat that chip off of your shoulder. Use this to get you there. Don't let them come and steal what belongs to you. Get up! Go get your joy back!

Change is a good spice to life. It's often difficult to add due to the unknown; yet it's necessary. My friend, don't despair. You're hungry. Stop starving yourself of life. Let *The* Great Spirit feed you. He's stirring the pot and adding His flavor. He's going to turn it all around for your good. God's going to stir it up. He's going to take perversion and turn it around. He's going to take addiction and turn it around. He's going to take rage and turn it around. He's going to take pain and turn it around. He's going to take disobedience and turn it around. Yes. He's going to take selfishness and turn it around. Let Him do it for you my friend. Get out of the way. It's never too late for Him to stir in His flavor.

You may say: "I can't forgive them. You don't know what they did to me. You don't know how they hurt me." Or, "I don't know how to forgive. I can't." God says: "Put it in the pot and let go." He says: "Don't touch it! I cannot be burned nor bruised"

Hot Pot

My friend, there's no hope without forgiveness. You're not *their* victim. Say it! I _____am not a victim anymore - I am a victor. I forgive all those who've ever wronged me; including myself. I am going to let go. I'm going to put all my troubles in the pot.

Friends, if you filled in the blank above with your name; God's stirring the pot for you. *The* Great Spirit's adding flavor. He's making sure the end result is *M'm! M'm! Good!* He's making sure there's no bitter or spoil. He's turning sour milk into cheese and yogurt: bitter fruit into fine wine. My friend, taste and see that He is good.

He's already preserved your destiny. No obstacle is going to spoil it. *The* Great Spirit has sealed the lid, who can open it? He's prepared a table for you. Yes. *The* Great Spirit's working in your kitchen. Yes. He's preparing good things for you. What God's stirring in the pot isn't for mama, daddy, sister, brother - it's for you. It's for your nourishment: to be health unto your bones. Yum! Yum! It smells like hope and tastes like favor; but, it's grace seasoned with mercy.

You've made up your mind. You've said in your heart: "This doesn't belong to me. God promised me something better. I'm not going to let what the enemy has done to me stop me. I'm not going to let my circumstances define who I am. I'm not going to eat from a bent spoon of negativity. I'm not going to let discouraging words spoil my appetite. I know who I am. I'm a child of God. My *Father* will provide for me."

You no longer have a, "*he done this she done that*" attitude. You say instead, "It is done." Or, "All is well." You no longer say, "*I can't do this, I can't do that.*" No. You say, "I can do all things..." You no longer sing: "*if only this if only that.*" No. Sounds of praise vibrate from your lips. Your emotions are no longer moved by the enemy. You remember: "Greater is He that is in you, than he that is in the world." You no longer feel the need to pick up that hot pot. No. You realize, God's a better cook than you'll ever be.

Maybe your family's falling apart. Maybe your children are continuously placing their hands on hot iron. Maybe you're too stressed to know what's best. You feel as though you can't afford to trust again - like you can't afford to love again. My friend, the fat around your heart is too thick; throw it in the pot. It can be added for flavor. You don't have to worry. You do not have to be afraid. God knows what to do with every ingredient of your life. Throw it in the pot. Wait patiently for dinner to be served.

We've all done and said things we're not proud of. You may think what you've done is too great to be forgiven. You may think it'll only add stones to your pot. Little dove, God's already forgiven you; you just have to forgive yourself We're human: we don't truly know our Spirit; but, our flesh we know well - this is why we're conflicted. My friend, God can turn those stones in your life to bread.

The Great Spirit wants you to throw something in the pot. He has not given up on you. Why do you give up on yourself? He has a plan for your life. Everything God has promised you is going to come to pass. Are you listening to the right voice?

A good voice doesn't discourage; it encourages a man to do the things most beneficial for the spirit. God's in the kitchen preparing a full course dinner for you: wait patiently at the table. Supper will be delicious. Your blessings will be served on time.

"Well everything you're saying sounds good; but God aint gone forgive me for what I did. I've done terrible things." My friend, lift your eyes from the ground. Be of good cheer. God saves whom He chooses. He stirred the pot for Saul, turned things around to make Paul; what then can He not do for you?

I remember a story about a man who divided his property between two sons. The older son stayed close to his father; but the younger son, gathered all his inherited wealth and moved to a faraway land. Yes. He was having fun living wild and free. He squandered money.

There was famine in all the land. The young man had to hire himself out to a citizen. One day he began to hunger while feeding pigs. Then, "He longed to fill his stomach with the pods that they were eating, but no one gave him anything."

When the young man thought about what he was doing, he said: "Wait a minute. My father's servants have enough food to spare, and here I am starving to death. I will go back home to my father and say to him: Father I've sinned against heaven and against you. I am no longer worthy to be called your son; make me like one of your hired servants."

Hot Pot

As the young man approached, his father saw him from a long distance and rejoiced. "He ran to his son, threw his arms around him, and kissed him." The young man began to recite his speech as planned. "Father, I've sinned against heaven and against you. I am no longer worthy to be called your son." The father said nothing to the young man. He was too busy ordering his servants to care for him. "Quick! Bring the best robe and put it on him. Put a ring on his finger and sandals on his feet. Bring the fattest cow and kill it. Let's have a feast and celebrate. For this son of mine was dead, and is alive again; he was lost and is found."

When the older brother arrived and observed, he became angered. He refused to go into the celebration. He said to the father: "Look! All these years I've been slaving for you. I've never disobeyed you. And you never even gave me a young goat. But when the son of yours who's squandered your property with prostitutes comes home; you kill the fattest calf for him!" The father replied, "My son you are always with me, and everything I have is yours. But we had to celebrate and be glad, because this brother of yours was dead and is alive again; he was lost and is found."

You may have taken everything God's given you and squandered it. You may have left His house to go to a strange land: to do wicked things. Go home to your father. He can see you in the distance. He knows your heart. He knows your needs. He knows you're dirty. He wants to clean, clothed, and feed you.

What you did isn't going to matter. He's going to order His servants to provide for you. Yes. God will prepare a feast for you. If you're dead; let these words of hope resurrect you. If you're lost; follow the light home.

When you decide to let go of the hot pot, a world of new opportunities will open up for you. I speak from experience; having clutched unforgiveness myself. These aren't just words spilling over; it's my heart and soul pouring out to you from a pot well done: from a portion of a full course meal God's prepared for me. I want to share with you.

Headed to a women's shelter to make donation, I was in a radiant mood. Nonetheless, my gas hand was on empty. I stopped at a nearby station to fill up. While I was there, I noticed the pump didn't say regular unleaded. I thought to myself: *Well this is strange; I'll ask the lady behind me if she knows which is which.* All the pumps seemed to say the same thing; but, I needed to be sure.

When I inquired of the woman she ignored me the first time. She continued to pump her gas rolling her eyes. If looks could kill; I would certainly be dead. I could feel myself getting annoyed with her attitude. However, I decided to give her the benefit of doubt. I decided to ask her again. Thinking maybe she didn't hear me the first time. Maybe she wasn't rolling her eyes at me.

Excuse me, ma'am. Do you know which button is regular unleaded? "I Don't Know!" She yelled - throwing her hands up in the air. My heart jumped. I couldn't understand her reaction to my simple question.

I needed gas. I walked back over to my pump and pushed the button with the lowest price. I could feel something began to stir up inside of me. It wasn't good. I thought: *why do people treat me this way? How do I respond to them?* I heard two words: "Bless them."

It took me awhile to get into the car. Something was being taken from me. I wanted it back. I debated if I wanted to say anything else to the already irritated women; but I had to put my ego aside. I'm an empath. If I didn't say anything, I would've carried that negative experience in my heart for hours, weeks, maybe even years. I would've let the enemy steal my joy.

I walked over close enough, hoping she'd see the smile on my face. *Thank you. God bless you.* I could see the shame in her demeanor as she responded, "you too." I didn't do it for her. I did it for me. It wasn't said to manipulate her into feeling guilty. It was said to take back something that belonged to me. At that moment, I decided not to pick up the hot pot; and God provided me with a cool handle. I decided to forgive. For the first time in my life, I was in control of my own emotions. It felt good.

Maybe you've crossed paths with an angry pump lady. Maybe it was the cashier at the grocery store; or, the driver with road rage. Let go of the hot pot. Yes. My friend, let God provide you with a cool handle.

Too often we think the battle belongs to us. Too often we think we're the creator of fire. We think we're in control of the end results. No. We're only in control of our actions. We're only in control of the choices we make in response to situation and circumstance.

Hot Pot

Don't let anyone steal your joy - take it back and invite them to dinner. You'll burn yourself holding onto negative responses. You'll limit yourself by thinking: "All people are going to treat me this way. Maybe I'm a bad person. I'm not meant to be happy. I should just stop trying. I should just give up." No. Take your life back. Demand your victory. If you hold unforgiveness in your heart: it will burn. It'll leave scars; too many and you'll become unidentifiable.

My friend, I have good news. God's handling the hot pot for you. God is standing in your kitchen. Yes. He's cooking up something good. Where you'd be hot; He doesn't even break a sweat. Where you'd create a big mess; He always keeps it clean. Where you'd have mixed matched shapes and jagged edges; His words alone are sharp enough to cut through; and His love makes everything equal.

Yes. God has a celebration planned for you. He's already chosen the theme. He's sent out invitations. He's planned the menu. He's knows the playlist. He's cleaned the crystal, china, and silver. Yes. God our GOD is cleaning house.

My friend, *The* Great Spirit's taken inventory; He's made a detailed shopping list of your needs. Everything is on schedule. He's already set the stage for your success. He's made a place for you to hang your coat. There's a seat at His table with your name on it. Yes. The table has been set. My love, if you look; you'll see the beautiful arrangement. The candles are lit, the wine is uncorked; the bread is on the table. Now, God's waiting for you to arrive.

Maybe you don't know how close to *The* Great Spirit you are. You don't know how much He cares for you. You're blinded by unforgiveness. You rather believe He can't do the impossible. You'd rather believe your dreams will never come true. You'd rather settle where you are and not accept where you're going. My friend, you've put a wall up around you. You refuse to let anyone in. You've been holding that hot pot for too long. Let it go!

Maybe you were doing fine until you *did this*. Maybe you were doing fine until you *did that*. Maybe you were doing fine until you *met him*. Maybe you were doing fine until you *met her*. My friend, none of that matters - it happened; but it doesn't matter.

Love is what matters. Forgiveness matters. You fell down into a pit where God placed a ladder. Climb out of darkness back into the light. Get up! Don't let a lie win the race. Don't keep trying to hold onto that hot pot. No. Tell yourself right now and do it: "I'm going to let this go."

A key ingredient used by *The* Great Spirit is called forgiveness. What's forgiveness? In definition: it's the intentional and voluntary process, by which the offended undergoes emotional change regarding an offense by letting go. Yes. By letting go of negative emotions held against the offender - such as hate. Once you've completed this process, without seeking vengeance or wishing harm to come to the wrongdoer; you've successfully forgiven. My friend, it's not yours. Release it!

You've been sick for a long time. You've been walking in shame. Hold your head up high. There's a party being prepared in your honor. God's cooking up something good for you. It's going to be delicious. Yes. Grace is in the pot and mercy is on your plate. My friend, because you've decided to let it go: there's healing going on in your body right now. Yes. *The* Great

Spirit's stirring the pot. He's turning that medical report around.

You've lost your job because of rumors. There was a snake in the grass close to you. It manipulated you - it was jealous. It wanted what you had. You decided to let *The* Great Spirit provide you with a cool handle. Guess what? God's turning things around for you. He's caught the snake and placed it in your pot. Yes. Things will turn around for your good: to work in your favor; to fatten you in the spirit, and provide milk for your faith.

"Where was this Great Spirit when I was being raped? Where was this Great Spirit when I was being beaten? Where was this Great Spirit when I was abandoned and left with nothing? Where was He when my loved one was being murdered?"

He was in the kitchen. He was handling a hot pot. He was cooking for you. He was already turning things around. Forgive him.

When we were children our parents did things we didn't understand. They had ways we did not know. They took things from us; then, gave things to us. They told us no; then, told us yes. They warned us from experience of danger. When we burned, bruised, or scrapped our flesh; they were there to doctor our wounds: all these things they did to protect and keep us safe. They sacrificed so that we could have more. This is the same for God.

You may have been hurt. Maybe you're still in shock. You don't know what happened. You've been at your lowest point in life. Maybe you're still stuck in disbelief. Maybe things don't make sense to you. You struggle every day to get out of bed. You're numbed by pain and panicked by fear. You don't know where to start; or how much you have left. My friend, forgive and let go of the hot pot.

Sure, the pit is deep; but you've been provided a way out. There's nothing wrong with being down for a little while. It's okay to grieve. It's okay to mourn. It's a natural part of life. It's good for healing. You cannot dress a wound you don't know exists. Sometimes, we have to go to a place to face what lurks in the dark; to see what we cannot see topside: to know what lies on *both sides of the fence.* My friend, make sure you know where the stairs are to get back up.

I know you think you're not getting anywhere. Nevertheless, when you forgive; you'll get past the debris, and your territory will be enlarged. Things take time to develop. If you rush this development, it will not turnout the way it should. You may forget an important ingredient for the desired outcome. If you let it sit too long: it will spoil. Or, you allow another to sneak in and steal what belongs to you. You cannot rush time; nor can you get time wasted back. Focus on you. If it's meant to be; it will be. If not, then let what will *be - be*.

Either way my friend, you're going to be alright. Don't lose your focus. Forgive them. Yes. Forgive yourself. Stay grounded. There's nothing you can do right now to fix this situation. You've done enough. You've cried enough. You've prayed enough. It's going to take divine assistance. Like time, it's out of your control; and my friend at this point: it should be out of your hands. GET YOUR HANDS OFF OF IT! Once you do this, what needs to be done - can be done.

Unforgiveness is the greatest obstacle you'll ever have to overcome. Forgiveness is the greatest task to complete. When your *I don't care(s)* and *I hate you(s)* are consolidated to: *I love you*; you'll find rest and peace.

Hot Pot

Forgiveness like love is a choice that comes from within. Search the various regions of your heart. Do you forgive?

If your answer to the question is no; don't be afraid, guilty, or ashamed. It doesn't mean you're a bad person. No. It means there's work to do. I don't know anyone who can do the job better than God. Do you? Let Him know you need His help. Let Him know you can't do it on your own. Let Him know you're willing to forgive. You just don't know how. He'll show you the way. Let Him know you're hungry. He'll feed you.

I'm not here to beat you down; or, tell you that you're going to hell. Truth is, I don't know. That's not my purpose in life. My calling is to encourage, to inspire, and to love. I'm not going to throw my Bible at you no matter what I believe I think I know. I get it. I've been there. I've done that. Now, I love. Now, I and the Light are one. I found the stairs. I know the way out. I dropped that hot pot. It took me years but I did it.

My heart was scarred; but, it was healed. I didn't know who I was anymore. I'd changed so much. I was disgusted with myself. I held onto that hot pot so long I was scared to look in the mirror. One day, I realized I wasn't feeling pain at all. I was feeling at fault. I was feeling guilt and shame. No. Not pain. The pain stopped long ago. I was self-afflicting blame.

God didn't give up on me. He said: "Let go. Come sit down at my table. You need to eat. Let me feed you." I said: *But God he did that and she done this. He said this and they took that. I can't let go. I don't know how.* He responded, "Trust in me with all your heart. For I know the plans I have for you, they are for good and not evil, to give you a future and a hope." Oh, my dear friends, "Trust in Him at all times...pour out your hearts to Him, for He is your refuge.

If I could lose my mind and *The* Great Spirit helped me find it; He can help you find forgiveness and love in your heart. If He could pick up the pot for me; why can't He do the same for you? If He can stir things up in my life for good and not evil; what makes you think He's not turning things around for you? I'm no less or greater than you. When I pinch my flesh: it hurts. Yes. When I tear my flesh: it bleeds.

I dream of your future. Overcome. *The* Great Spirit has enough utensils to supply not some of your needs; all your needs. He has things stored up in His cabinets for you. He knows what to add to make the bitter circumstances in your life taste sweet.

Remember my love, in your darkest hour; the light of God will appear great. Will you open your eyes to gaze upon such glory? Or, will you close them in immature defeat?

The heart of a man is a temple in which the sun rises from and sets again; with love, it's forever shinning; with forgiveness, it entertains hope. I beseech you my dears to forgive today; because tomorrow may be too late. Let Go! Let It Go!

The issues of your heart carry much weight on the outcome of your life. What are you carrying around with you? What are you holding onto? Does it benefit you after it's all said and done? Is it helping you to be the best of you? Or, is it weighing you down; holding you back from opportunity?

Time has passed my friends. Good energy has been wasted. What you do in this moment can provide sustenance to the spirit; which fuels the fire from within. Drop that hot pot. Throw in all negativity. Throw in your doubt. Throw in your fear. Throw in your shame. Let your worries be stirred to work in your favor. Let your problems be cooked till they're well done. Come sit down at the King's table. You've debated with yourself long enough. Your flesh was to victory for but a moment: the battle is not over. There's still a war to be won. Yes. Victory belongs to you my friend; but first, you must surrender. You must first let go of the hot pot. Let go, so healing can begin.

If you must hold onto to something; hold on to the light, and truth. They will guide you on your journey of being. Yes. They'll aid your cause and purpose in life. My friend, hold onto love and never let go: it will not rot, stain, nor stench. Unforgiveness; however, has an unpleasant fragrance: it makes a pot of chitterlings smell better than honeysuckle, and leaves a mark on everything it touches. It will break a person down until there's nothing left. Its negative energy will consume a life to the point of death.

Little dove, there's more for you. Where you are is not the end of the road - lesson you choose to give up. If you choose to build a wall on the path traveled; how will you ever know what lies on the other side? How could you ever see success in the distance? How can you ever find the truth? How will you ever arrive at the door of destiny to unlock it?

The good outweighs the bad. If your start has been full of bad things; your finish holds the good stuff. How much good stuff you acquire, depends on how far you're willing to travel down the path. You'll need strength to carry on. This is why *The* Great Spirit's cooking for you. My friend, let go and throw all that's holding you back into the pot. Lighten your load. Yes. Lay down your burdens and rest. You'll need energy to make it to where you're going.

It's okay to talk to yourself. Tell yourself: "I'm ready to move on from this. I'm equipped with everything I need. I'm not alone. My life matters. I'm beautifully and wonderfully made. I'm worthy. I deserve to be loved. My greater is coming. I will not be afraid anymore of the darkness - I am light. I'm going to love in spite of. I'm dropping the hot pot. I'm throwing everything holding me back into it. I want to heal. I'm ready to become. *Self* get out of my way!"

What you tell yourself is important. When you tell yourself what you're going to do; or, who you are, *self* listens and takes note. If you tell yourself positive uplifting things; you'll attract and display those things. If you say negative things to and about yourself over and over again; you'll act out.

Positive statements about *you* will keep your insides clean. Negative statements; however, will spread like mold and infest. Instead of telling yourself; "I'm nothing." Throw that insecurity in the pot and start telling yourself; "I'm enough." Be aware of what's playing on repeat inside of you. Yes. Be willing to change a broken record.

It's beneficial to know when to hold on, and when to let go. As a young girl, I loved to play on merry-go-rounds. My brother, Deek, would push me as fast as he possibly could. I'd wrap myself around the poles and squeeze tight. I knew I had to hold on. When everything around me stopped spinning; I knew it was time to get off. I had to let go to move on.

This is the lesson I've learned from struggle: when everything in life begins to spin out of control; hold on a little while longer. Don't give up. Have faith. When things stop spinning; it's okay to let go. It's over now.

Hot Pot

My friend, "To everything there is a season, and a time to every purpose under the heaven: a time to be born, and a time to die; a time to plant, and a time to pluck up that which is planted; a time to kill, and a time to heal; a time to break down, and a time to build up; a time to weep, and a time to laugh; a time to mourn, and a time to dance; a time to cast away stones, and a time to gather stones together; a time to embrace, and a time to refrain from embracing; a time to get, and a time to lose; a time to keep, and a time to cast away..." Do you know what time it is?

It's Time To Let Go

As long as we have hope,

we have direction, the energy to move,

and the map to move by

Hong Kong Proverb

Chapter Five:
Time Will Tell

My mama never asked me if I was lying about anything. No. She'd simply say, "Time will tell." At first, I didn't grasp the meaning - until ole Time started running his mouth. He began to tell it all. He didn't hold nothing back. I thought he was a curse; but I later found Time to be my best friend.

Have you ever tried to explain the truth until you turned blue in the face? That's a lot of explaining when you're a person of color. There've been times when I nearly explained myself to death. No joke. What I did, when I did, how I did, why I did, my intent, my purpose, my calling, my dress, my walk, my talk. A few years back, I realized I was wasting my breath.

Time knows you better than you know yourself. Only *The* Great Spirit can win a debate against him. He's all seeing, all knowing, and has no problem with telling all your business. What you do in the dark will come to the light with time. If someone has accused you to be something or someone you're not, "Time will tell." If someone has wronged you and it appears they're going to get away with it. Don't worry about it: "Time will tell." If you're put on this earth to do good and not evil; or the opposite, "Time will tell." If you do not know your enemy, "Time will tell." If you're lost and confused, "Time will tell."

You don't have to explain who you are to anyone. You may feel the need. You may want to sing the song of explanation: *"Well, I only did it because..., I do it because..., I was just trying to..., no, no, no, I was just saying..., No. Please wait! Let me explain."* But when it comes down to the nature of who you are put on this earth to be; there's no explanation required. It's better to explain these things with your actions and not your mouth. You can show them better than you can tell them. Save your words. Let time do the telling.

Though you may tell, many will not listen; and though you speak, many will not hear: and those who hear will hear what it is they desire to hear. You my love, are like a rose in a garden of rocks. I gaze upon your beauty. You're set apart for a reason. *The* Great Spirit has done great things in your future. He's removed the limitations of man. You're free to be. Man may have the power to chain you in manipulation - if you let him; but *The* Great Spirit will break each and every one of those chains.

You do not need man to validate you. You're validated by God: *The* Creator, *The* Most High, the ruler of all things above and below - *The* Great Spirit. He's not limited by the issues of man. My friend, don't carry the weight cut from around your neck. Let it go. It would be as if you're freed from slavery, yet chose to remain a slave. The problem is not with the choice: it's with limitation and fear. You don't owe anything. The cost has been paid. Do you understand you don't owe them an explanation? Do you understand you don't owe them and excuse?

The Lord is my example. As he was being persecuted, he said only but a few words. The Governor asked, "Art thou the King of the Jews?" Jesus responded, "Thou sayest." The governor was confused. He couldn't understand why after hearing what the chief priests and elders were saying - all that they accused Jesus of; why Jesus kept silent. Pilate asked, "Hearest thou not how many things they witness against thee?" Jesus didn't speak a word.

What the Governor didn't understand: Jesus wasn't there to win a battle. No. He knew the battle was already won. Jesus was there to become. Pilate didn't want to crucify Jesus. He said, "Why, what evil hath he done?" But the crowd wanted to be entertained by blood and screamed: "Crucify him." Even now, man will crucify man with the tongue for sport.

Those who believe there's no God; try to play God. They want the control. They'll try to intimidate you. They want you to forget who you are. They will try to keep you steps behind. They will try to keep you beneath and below. Some are not willing to share with you. They want it all. Others, once they've received; will ration what was free to them for high price. You may ask, "Who are *they*?" My answer is: *they* know who *they* are. And though their intentions are currently hidden from you; with time you'll know them all by name. Yes. Time will point them out to you - "Time will tell."

If you have faith, you don't have to prove it. When you truly believe, you don't have to claim it. There's a bit of truth to be told in silence - a whisper of *I Am*. The sun doesn't debate with the sky of its existence.

My friend, take heed, the stomach of man is never satisfied; it will be filled to hunger again. You can explain your life away; but, *they* will seek your bones also. Do you understand? You have nothing to prove. Just be!

Don't worry about what they're saying. It won't matter. I promise. Their words will not be able to reach as high as you're going. This is all about your growth my love. Use it the right way, for the right reason. Don't waste your time. Think, concentrate, communicate, create, and inspire. Continue to be optimistic about it. Continue to be the fun loving person you are. Continue to put a smile on the face of others with your sense of humor. Continue to enjoy life. You've been given something special: don't waste it. They've been given something special - you. I woe and pity them that take advantage of such a gift. It's sad - not for you; but for them.

Maybe you're being judged by the standards of your past. It's not always easy to ignore the wind; especially, when it's slamming doors and breaking windows. It's not always easy to believe you're special when people tell you every day you're nothing. When people make you feel as though you have no value.

Yes. People tell you every day you don't have what it takes: You don't have the talent; you don't have the look; you don't have the education: "Look at you; you're dumb, just plain ole stupid, and aint nobody ever gone be willing to hire no nut." They call you a fool; kick you while you're down; throw stones at you: and spit in your face. My friend, hold your head up high. Time can and will prove them wrong.

Don't let what people say about you keep you from you. You're going to be just fine. Your success in life is not measured by their words; but by your works, and spirit. If people aren't willing to support you on your journey; if they aren't willing to drive you there: get out of the car and walk on your own two feet. I know it's in you. I know you have what it takes. You can do it. You can make it. You'll get there. But my faith in you my friend is not enough.

No. What you need is time. Give yourself time. You'll increase in value. A man has many discoveries; but *The* Great Spirit lays the mark to be found. You are one to be found my love. It was never meant for you to be hidden. In time, all the debris and particle covering will be removed. People will talk about how bright you shine from a faraway distance. *The* Great Spirit has not brought you this far to leave you; *His sheep,* in the hands of wolves. He will not leave His treasure in the den of thieves.

It's with time the ignored bud becomes the gazed upon flower. You'll blossom. Be confident in your works of love. Save the amount of time you'd be using trying to convince others of your good nature to nurture. You cannot change the way that person thinks or feels about you - no matter how hard you try. It's not you *they* hate; *they* hate the God in you. We can only change ourselves and our way of thinking.

It has been written: "Then Moses said to God, "If I come to the people of Israel and say to them, 'The God of your fathers has sent me to you,' and they ask me, 'What's His name?' what shall I say to them?" God said to Moses, "*I Am* who *I Am*." And He said, "Say this to the people of Israel, '*I Am* has sent me to you." God also said to Moses, "Say this to the people of Israel, 'The Lord, the God of your fathers, the God of Abraham, the God of Isaac, and the God of Jacob, has sent me to you.' This is my name forever, and thus I am to be remembered throughout all generations." The same goes for you salt of the earth; you are who you are, and I am who I am: because we are.

Your attitude should be: "I know what they say about me, but I'm not going to let it stop me. I hear them calling me names, but I'm not going to let it get me down. I know that I am. I know *The* Great Spirit has not brought me this far to leave me. I'm going to be the best I can possibly be as man. I'm going to do the best I can possibly do being flesh. I'm not here to please man; I'm here to get closer to God. I'm here to become."

If you keep your focus on the road ahead, you cannot be distracted by what follows behind. Keep your eyes on the prize and continue to move towards it. My friend, you're shielded by God. Man's weapons cannot even put a dent in your armor. A scratch to your breastplate can be wiped away like chalk on a board. Your helmet is made of precious metal never known by the hands of a blacksmith. Your shield goes before you, your belt restrains, your sword delivers, and your shoes testify the way. You're fully covered from head to toe: shinning in glory. No. Don't worry about what people say: "Time will tell."

My friend, you're lovely. You're loved and favored by *The* Great Spirit. Let them laugh at you. Let them call you names. Time will tell them who you really are. Don't worry about your talent. Don't worry about not being good enough. You'll have what you need - when you need. You don't have to explain your blessings. You don't need to cover your gifts. Man did not give it, and man cannot take it away.

You're the chosen one - *The* King's favorite. Walk with your head held high in the truth of your existence. I've learned: if you let time tell; you'll win every debate. You're like a tree in which the birds come to rest. Even the rodents will find shelter and warmth in you.

You see my friend; your talent surpasses them all - because you love. No. Not just your close friends and family. You truly love even your enemies. "You bless those that curse you, and do good to those that hate you. You pray for them that despitefully use you, and those that persecute you." Our brother once said, "Behold, what manner of love the Father hath bestowed upon us, that we should be called the sons of God: therefore the world knoweth us not, because it knew Him not." My friend, "Time will tell."

I know you get angry. Sometimes you're disappointed. You get frustrated. Your heart shatters. Sometimes you become fearful. Why not? You're flesh and bone. You have feelings. Words can cut deep. Feeling misunderstood can wake you from a dream. My friend, go to your quiet place. Continue to work. Go better your skill. Let time change what you cannot. Let time be your witness. They'll continue to persuade each other's minds with thoughts of evil against you; but they can do no harm to the will of *The* Great Spirit. It's you that's purposed for the moments to come. You in which they are warned: "Touch not mine anointed, and do my prophets no harm." Know who you are my love. Arise, great leader. Dust yourself off!

When you change your response, they'll change their approach. My friend, watch from the sideline as *The* Great Spirit intervenes and tackles the issue. Stop trying to fight a war that's not your war to fight. The battle doesn't belong to you. Why stand on the battlefield? Why give them what they want? Why show them what they're looking for? They seek to find your weakness. The mob is out for blood. They want to kill, steal, and destroy. They're not expecting to run into *The* Great Giant. They're expecting you to march to the beat of their drums; but oh does time have a surprise for them. Time is going to tell it! Time is going to tell them who victory belongs to. Victory belongs to you.

No. Don't waste time trying to explain what you don't know. Don't waste time trying to convince others of the good nature of your character. Don't waste time trying to impress people who do not like you - because of some vain thing.

If they don't like you at your worst; they can't possibly love you at your best. If they weren't there for you when you were down; don't pull them up to you when you get higher in life: lessen you fall back down – or they push you down to take your place.

My love, take the time for you. Take the time for your breakthrough. Take the time to get ready for your bountiful harvest. Take the time to be thankful of constant flow. Pray others go into the house to be lathered by God.

When you stop allowing people to intimidate you, you'll experience a peace from within. A sudden sensation of positive creative energy will explode in your life. You'll become a better leader, a better teacher, a better entertainer, a better communicator, a better lover, and a better friend.

Start thinking: "They look good; but God looks better. They sound good; but God sounds better. They run fast; but, God runs faster." It's important for you to understand that people are not perfect. Anything *you, they, he, she, or it* can do, *The* Great Spirit can do better.

Time is the best fortuneteller; he never predicts the future wrong. When people tell you: "You'll never be able to get over that divorce. You'll never be able to find a better job. You'll never be able to graduate from school. You'll never be able to walk again. You'll never be able to overcome that addiction." Or, "You'll never be able to get a record deal - you can't sing. You'll never be able to get a book published - you can't write. You'll never be able to buy a house - you can't afford it." Step out of the way. Let time do the telling. Don't believe them. They're predicting your future wrong.

Where there's God's will, there's your way. As long as you're willing, God is able. Let your faith go beyond the boundaries. Speak only what you want to existence. Give ear to what will propel you forward: not what will leave you stranded behind.

It's easy to think: "Maybe their right. Maybe I can't do it. Maybe I won't make it. It'll never happen for me. I don't think I'm equipped. I don't have what it takes. I should just stop trying." No my friend. Don't stop trying. Don't give up. If *The* Great Spirit's placed a drive inside of you; you're going somewhere.

Get the bug out of your ear. Focus. Stop letting people discourage you with their disbelief in your ability. Stop letting them control you with their fear and failures. Discouraging people you encounter are not happy in life. Remember my friend, "Misery loves company." They don't want you to be happy. Their lives are filled with negativity. They cannot see the steps in front of them. They're threatened by you. They think you want what they have. Many are jealous; they want what you have - others speak to be speaking. Don't allow them to dangle you around as their puppet. No. Know who you are. Expect things to work in your favor. Proceed to your destiny. Arrive! Become! Let time tell your future.

You don't need their support to become; nor do you need their permission to succeed. It is okay for you to want it; but, it's important you understand you don't need it. Whether people support you or not; it's best you try. In today's time, it's unlikely to hit a home run if you never swing the bat. How can you become a dancer if you never take the time to dance? How can you become a cook when you're afraid of fire? How will you succeed, when you're afraid to fail?

Do not fill your life with regret. Do not allow yourself to be hunted by *what if*. If you have an idea that doesn't go away without returning; it's worth perusing. If you have a dream you don't easily wake up from; it's worth making a reality.

If you'll let time do the telling; if you'll stop allowing yourself to be intimidated, and start expecting

The Great Spirit to show up and show out in your life: He'll wipe the smirk off of their faces. He did it for Joseph, and He'll do the same for you. When you let time do the telling, you don't have to worry about nothing. No. You'll be too busy expecting. You'll be too busy expecting things to work out the way they should: for your good and in your favor - according to your faith and the will of God.

I'm asking you to let time tell. Have faith beyond the boundaries of now. See the knots out of the rope. Use what people say about you to add fuel to the fire. Do not settle for the expectations of others. Don't let intimidation or manipulation hold you back from becoming the best you. Give things time in your life to develop like the fetus in the womb. Stop letting your mind take inventory of your failures. Instead, let your heart take inventory of your successes. Stop worrying about what other people say about you. Start believing what God is saying to you.

Growing up I was talk about. I was called *"nappy headed."* I was told I'd never make it; I wasn't educated enough. I was told I could never be a writer - I didn't know how to dot my I's or cross my T's. I was told

I'd never graduate high school. I was said to be *"too skinny."* When I gained weight, I was told that I was *"too fat."* I was pushed down on my face; but, each time I got back up – crying; but that's not my point.

My point is: you can never fully satisfy the stomach of a man. People will always have something to say about the choices you make in life. You'll always have people who whisper behind your back; or, lie to your face. My Example once said, "For John the Baptist came neither eating bread nor drinking wine; and ye say, He hath a devil. The Son of man is come eating and drinking; and ye say, behold a gluttonous man, and a winebibber, a friend of publicans and sinners!" My dear friends, "Wisdom is justified of all her children." Time will tell.

If I knew then what I know now, I'd let time tell my future. I wouldn't have felt the need to fight a battle already won. I would've saved my words for someone who cared. I would've walked away towards my future, leaving negativity behind eating my dust. I would've believed I'd already arrived the moment *The* Great Spirit told me I would. Then, I didn't give things time; now, time demands it.

My friend, I know you're afraid you'll be left alone. People try to talk you out of doing the right thing. People try to talk you out of doing what you must do for you. They try to control you by saying: "I won't be your friend *if...*; I will go *if...*; or, "I can't ___ *if...*" My friend, save your: *Well, I only did it because...; I do it because...; I was just trying to..., no, no, no, I was just saying..., No. Please wait! Let me explains.* Time is demanding you get to work in your life.

It's not too late for you my friend. You've not run out of time. The clock's still ticking. Every second, every minute, every hour; depends on what you choose to do with time. Do you choose to waist it on vain debates? Do you choose to spend your time trying to explain yourself to others? Do you choose to spend your time watching others step on your ideas and crush your dreams? Or, do you choose to be empowered by *The* Great Spirit? Do you choose to be inspired? Encouraged? Do choose to take the time to develop your talent? Do you choose to take the time to prototype that idea? Do you choose to take the time to become? Do you choose to let time tell your future?

Did you make the right choice? My friend, "Time will tell."

Walk In Integrity Of Existence.

Chapter Six:
Pull the Reins

I like the story about a man named Balaam and his donkey. To make a long story short: as the man and the donkey were traveling a path with two servants, the donkey saw an angel in the road holding a sword. The donkey sensed danger and turned off of the road. Balaam began to beat her.

Every direction the donkey turned, the angel cut off the way. The donkey decided to lie down. The man kept beating his donkey. Finally, the donkey was able to speak: "What have I done to you, that you've struck me these three times?" Balaam responded, "Because you've made a fool of me. I wish I had a sword in my hand, for then I would kill you." "Am I not your donkey, on which you've ridden all your life long to this day?

Is it my habit to treat you this way?" "No." Balaam answered.

Suddenly, Balaam is able to see what the donkey see's and falls on his face. "Why have you struck your donkey these three times? Behold, I've come out to oppose you because your way is perverse before me, the donkey saw me and turned aside before me these three times, if she had not turned aside from me, surely just now I would have killed you and let her live." Then Balaam said to the angel, "I've sinned, for I did not know that you stood in the road against me. Now therefore, if it is evil in your sight, I will turn back."

In the same way, there may be something or someone blocking the path you're traveling - trying to motivate you to pull the reins. When things appear to go wrong in your life; when all you do seems to fail; consider, maybe you're going in the wrong direction. Maybe you're headed for destruction. *The* Great Spirit's trying to protect you. Maybe you're trying to collect rubies when you're supposed to be gathering diamonds.

Pull the Reins

Your life could be fine. Everything could be working out the way you want it to. You feel blessed; you sense your steps are guided, and suddenly things change. Suddenly, you're having problems on the job, become depressed - you can't seem to get that relationship back on track. Every time you try to get up, it feels like you're being pushed back down and sat on. You can't explain it. You didn't expect it. The donkey in your life turned off the road. My friend, you're going in the wrong direction. If you'll pull the reins and turn back; you'll find blessings waiting for you on a different path. Yes. There are opportunities waiting for you.

On the right path, you'll have the help you need when you need it. Things will line up. You'll find the right match. Your marriage is reconciled. Your sickness is healed. You'll no longer feel depressed. Things will fall into place. All because you've decided to pull the reins and turn back. You stopped beating the donkey. You're allowing the donkey in your life to carry you to safety.

You've gone your way long enough. It hasn't worked out for you. You've been hanging out with the wrong crowd long enough. It's put you on a dangerous path. You've been trying to marry the wrong man. Time after time, he's shattered your heart and stepped on the pieces. Consider your way, pull the reins, and turn back.

You won't have to look at the time. You won't have to consider your age. You won't have to settle for a seat on the ground. You may struggle right now in fear. Your mind shows you pictures of all the ways you'll fail; all the things that can happen to you -trying to talk you out of changing course. Don't let it win the debate. You feel like you're being smashed between a donkey and a hard place; don't let it get you down. Making the change is for your good. What do you have to lose that cannot be found again?

We have to look deeper into our situations to find the problem. You can see the table, but it's more than its surface and color. There are tiny particles you cannot see inside. *The* Table maker knows more about the table than you do. *The* Great Spirit's trying to lead you to a better path. He's trying to carry you to your destiny; but, you're constantly fighting Him. He says, "What have I done to you, that you suddenly do not trust me? Am I not your God, on which you have been relying all your life long to this day? Is the land not flowing with milk and honey? Are you not fed when you're hungry? Are you not provided with a spring to drink? Is it my habit to treat you this way? Have I not been fair in my dealings with you? Consider your way and pull the reins, for I know the plans I have for you...they are plans for good and not disaster, to give you a future and a hope."

Some of us have no problem with trying to force the hand of God. Then, when He gives us what we want: to show us our way isn't good; we blame Him for our failures. We stop believing in Him because we let ourselves down. We stop praying to Him because we're ashamed. We stop trusting in Him because we lose hope. We stop following Him because we've traveled so far up the road; we no longer see Him.

He doesn't carry you because you've made the choice to step off. Get back on. It's not meant for you to suffer. You weren't created to fail. There's more waiting for you in the other direction. You have unwrapped gifts and undiscovered talents; sitting there, waiting for you to turn back. There are people standing at the edge of the road waiting to meet you: to be of service on your journey. My friends, *The* Great Spirit wants to take you higher; but, there are no mountains in the direction some of you are going.

Consider your way, pull the reins, and turn back if you have to. Find the problem and fix it. You cannot bandage a wound you don't know exists. Examine your surroundings and see if it's good for your health and wellbeing. Balance your checkbook to see if there's something in your finances you've overlooked. Take an inventory of the people you call friends to see which ones are standing in your corner. Turn back. You don't have to suffer. You don't have to struggle to make ends meet. Break free from your addictions and bad habits. Find love in yourself and in others. There are overwhelming possibilities for you down the street and around the corner - the other way. You'll have options to choose from. There'll be forks in the road and each way will lead to good. It's beneficial to pull the reins.

Why do you limit yourself? Do you not fully understand your capabilities? Why must you continue to beat the donkey? Are you content? *The* Great Spirit wants to bless you but you will not let Him. He's throwing blessings to you; but you're not catching them. You're letting them fall to the ground to spoil. It's not too late to catch God's favor. It's not too late to catch your blessing. No. God won't stop throwing them because He loves you. Consider your way, pull the reins, and go catch the favor of God. Stop fighting. Surrender. Advance to the next stage of your life.

Reins are tools used for directional control, speed, and collection of a horse. Sometimes, it's necessary to slow down. When something is on your path trying to throw you off course, don't stop or go the other way - go around it. If it's not bothering you: don't bother it. Keep moving forward. But if your donkey all of a sudden refuses to continue in the direction you're going; turn completely around.

Pulling the reins is change. It will help improve your situation. It will give you room to grow. Change will help you discover what you could not see before; and learn what it is you need to know. Your life will improve when you consider your way, pull the reins, and turn back. You'll have a new beginning - a fresh start. You'll see things with a new set of eyes. My friend, get to the root of the problem. Figure out what's blocking the way; then move it.

Pull the reins. Stop thinking: "That's just too hard. What if I fail? It's impossible for me to do right now. I have a crappy job. There's no better way. I have to get it the best way I know how." No. Get over that fear and start thinking: "I'm ready to make a change. I'm ready to learn how to do new things. I'm ready to surrender my way to go God's way. He's never steered me wrong. He'll lead me to a path of righteousness. He'll help improve my situation. I know He'll propel me forward. I'm going to trust Him in spite of all negativity."

My friend, turn. Go get what belongs to you. Walk through the doors with your name on it. Be blessed by what lives inside. See yourself surrounded by goodies - surrounded by opportunities. See yourself going back to school and graduating with honors. See yourself buying that new house. See yourself driving that new car. What color is it? You've had a rough start due to weakness; nevertheless, you'll have a strong finish.

A retail store manager I know had been out of a job for a couple of years. She had an enjoyable position with her employer before; however, after a discrepancy, the company decided to let her go. Every day she'd sit at the computer to apply for new jobs; but, the results were all the same - no follow up call for the interview.

Things weren't looking good. Bills piled up as her unemployment ran out. I remember saying to her: *Do you know how I always seem to get the job? I bug them until they give it to me.* I encouraged her to call the company if the company didn't call her. I went further in encouragement. I told her the name of the company that would hire her on if she used my method. She made the call. Less than a week later she was hired on. She was able to finally get things back on track.

Two years later, the donkey in her life began to turn off the road. She'd been fired from that very same job. She asked me, "Why do bad things keep happening to me? Why can I never seem to get ahead?" She was frustrated and tired of trying. She would get a job then get fired not long after. She'd get evicted and be forced to live in cars, on the streets, or in hotels. A family member would get arrested and she'd have to pawn something to bail them out. Time after time she'd, "Rob Peter to pay Paul"- but that was part of the problem.

Truth is, she lost her job because she was caught stealing from the company; and her house because she was living above her means. She explained, "I only do things like that when I feel I'm losing control."

What happened? In this case, it would've benefited her to pull the reins. It would've benefited her to surrender to change. No. She made a choice to beat the donkey. Suddenly, she's stuck once again between a donkey and a hard place. God wanted to take her to a new level in life; but, she wouldn't allow Him to take her there. She wanted the control; so, the donkey laid down underneath her.

The Great Spirit was saying to her, "You can get off and go if you want to. I'll be right here waiting. You don't see what I see unless I show it to you. You don't know what I know less I tell it to you. Who convinced you you'd fail by letting me carry you? Who told you wouldn't arrive on time? Who told you your life now is a reflection of the best I have for you? No. I have more. *I am* a great river; step into me, and I will carry you to a place of rest from your struggle."

Friends, *The* Great Spirit wants you to live. There's danger on the road ahead. Can you not see the volcano erupting in the distance? Do you not feel the strong winds of the tornado? The barren city in the direction you're traveling, has been consumed by both fire and water; and now, it's faced with drought. Why do you choose to go your way?

Think about it: what do you want to accomplish in life? What will be the outcome of your accomplishment? Where will your decisions of today lead you tomorrow? Can you get where you want to be in life the way you're going? Are you ready to try a new way? Listen to God as He speaks to your heart. Consider your way, pull the reins, and turn back.

You might be in a dead-end relationship, following the wrong crowd, working at the wrong job; or, unemployed when you're supposed to be working. You might be addicted to hard drugs, selling your body, and suicidal. You might feel unaccomplished and incomplete. Maybe you've given up, let yourself go, become a hoarder; or, a sloth. You have a negative attitude towards life. My friend, it's time to make some changes. It's time to consider your way and pull the reins.

Your loved ones are waiting for you to make the right choices. They've done all they can possibly do to help you. They're feeling out of options. They're feeling like they've failed you in some way. They can't help you. They cannot make the change for you. Help yourself and turn back.

Start changing the way you think. Allow positivity to flow in your life. God's still where you left Him. Go get back on the donkey. Let the donkey in your life carry you to your destiny. That juvenile detention center is not meant for you. That jail is not your advance. That abusive and neglectful relationship is not your refuge. That gang is not your savior. My friend, it'll only deliver you to the grave. You may have people traveling down the road with you, making the danger ahead seem like a nice enjoyable fieldtrip; but, enjoyment is for a moment - sorrow comes after. I beseech you my dear, consider your way. Pull the reins. Turn back!

I know you've tried before and failed. I know you feel lonely. So far, you've lived a life full of hurt and disappointment. Some of you feel out of place. *The Great Spirit* knows. He feels it all. He has compassion for you. He wants to change your situation. Let Him change your situation. Make the right choices.

Our lives are planned out. Do you know what could happen if the plans are not followed? If a builder built a house without a blueprint, the house may not turn out the way it's supposed to. Something could be missed. The measurements could be wrong. The materials may not be durable. The house could fall the next day. This is the same for the plan God has for your life. He's positioned you even as a child to go through what you've gone through for a reason. You can overcome. Someone may need to hear your testimony. What you went through can help save the life of another.

The donkey laid down under you for a reason. You cannot see what she sees. It could be worse. Things could've gone wrong. You could've been dead; but, you're still breathing. You're not meant to be a victim. You're meant to become the victor. You aren't meant to go down the road of sorrow. You're pre destined to live a life of peace and everlasting joy. If you consider your way, pull the reins, and turn back; you'll see for yourself: there's nothing on the road to your salvation to lose - everything to gain.

Yes. You'll see your stream of constant flow when you travel down the road of destiny. Your scenery will change once you surrender. You'll see and witness great wonders. When your faith is tested; you'll pass with flying colors.

Choose to remain encouraged. Flip faith back on. Choose to be happy. Stop beating the donkey and surrender to change. Listen to the teacher. *The* Great Spirit wants to turn things around in your life. He wants to take you from the desert: to sit you in paradise. Go in peace my friend.

When you decide to make the change; when you decide to turn around while others continue to beat the donkey; people will not understand. Some will expect you to ask them for permission to change. Others will call you names, whisper behind your back, and lie to your face. Many will cut their eyes at you - give you dirty looks; pay them no mind. No. "Do not fear or panic or be in dread of them, for the Lord your God is He who goes with you to fight for you against your enemies, to give you the victory."

I've heard it all: "You're crazy, stupid, foolish, self-righteous, hyper religious, hypocrite, whore, bitch:"

all manner of nasty things when I decided to pull the reins. People would tell me, "I hate you. You think you're better than everyone else. I wish you were never born." No. They were just sharing their discomfort with my presence.

I never told them what I thought. I think about what *The* Great Spirit says to me and about me. He says, "*I am* yours, and *you are* mine. I have work for you to do. My sheep have been in the field unattended too long. Go look after them." I think about who I am in Him. Yes. I think about love on a much deeper level. Man didn't pave the road I walk on; I owe no fee, but I pay them no mind. I will run through and leap over.

My friend, others cannot keep you from what *The* Great Spirit has for you. Only you can do that with the choices you make. They may not like your decision to change; that's their problem to deal with. They may try to get in your way. No worries. When they see *The* Great Giant they'll move. They cannot hold you back - you do that in fear. The path for you has been cleared. The way has been established. Your journey higher is prepared. Surrender your way to travel the path to enlightenment. Pull the reins.

We've been given instruction from one who's traveled the road before us: "Be not conformed to this world: but be ye transformed by the renewing of your mind, that ye may prove what is that good, and acceptable, and perfect, will of God." What does this mean? It means not to follow the crowd to destruction. Consider your way. Change the way you think if necessary. My friend, ensure what you're doing, and where you're going; is part of *The* Great Spirit's blue print for your life.

You're not too far gone down the wrong road. You still have time to make a change. You still have time to consider your way, pull the reins, and turn back. Opportunities are still waiting for you. You're one turn away from your blessing. Go get what belongs to you.

I use to hang out with the wrong crowd. There were days we'd get *five finger discounts* from the local markets. My parents were good to me. I had everything I needed. My heart gets the best of me. I would steal to provide for other people's children. The first time I tagged along, I watched how things were done. I was taught how to pop tags and place things on my person without being noticed. I didn't think much of anything that day. I did what I was told and that was that.

The next day, getting into the car, I heard a soft whisper: "Don't go." I look around. There was no one behind me. I ignored the voice and went anyway. As we were almost done for the day, one of the girls wanted to make another stop. She went into the store alone; but did not come out that way. She'd been arrested for shoplifting. That didn't teach us a lesson. We were scheduled to make our rounds the following day. I heard the whisper again, "Don't go;" but, I decided to go anyway.

I didn't look or talk like the other girls. I stood out from the crowd. While placing merchandise on my person in the dressing room, the manager entered to have a one on one with me: "Why are you doing this? You don't have to do this. Put everything you've taken back and I will not call the police." She continued: "Just promise me you'll never do it again." I promised and she kept her word. The next day, I heard: "Don't go." It was loud and clear. I knew who was talking to me.

I thought to myself: *three strikes and you're out.*
I had a feeling something was going to go wrong. There
was a knock on the door. When it was time to go; I
was hesitant. My feet wouldn't move. I told my cousin
Gwen: *Wait! Don't open the door; tell them I have the
runs.* Then, I went and sat down on the toilet as if it
was true. I could hear the disappointment in their
voices. I felt bad. But I was scared. I couldn't shake the
feeling. Later that day, I found out all except the driver
had been arrested.

My friend, I was following the wrong crowd. I was
traveling in the wrong direction. *The* Great Spirit
showed me the error of my way; but, I refused to look. I
ignored His voice until He had no choice but to scream
at me. I beat the donkey till the angel appeared. I had
to consider my way. I had to realize the life I was trying
to live belonged to someone else. God had a better plan
for my life. I knew the moment I didn't get arrested;
God had His hands on me. He's molding me like clay.
Yes. He's positioning me like a chess piece. Things
could've gone wrong. I could've been locked up behind
bars with the rest of them. But I made the choice to go

God's way. I pulled the reins and turned back; and was blessed with freedom.

That's the way *The* Great Spirit works. He doesn't want you to fail. He constantly moves around to keep you out of harm's way. He places you between a donkey and a hard place to keep you safe. He screams loud when you don't hear the whisper. He loves you. Don't you know how much you're loved? Turn around to see what a King has prepared for a servant. Witness His grace and mercy. It's sufficient for you.

My friend, if God's screaming at you, it's best you listen. If your donkey starts acting up, it's best you consider your way. Pull the reins. You're deserving of a good life. Turn around and face it. What do you have to lose? Are you happy right now? Do you believe you can progress the way you're going? Surrender to change. Commit to becoming the best of you. Commit to the journey higher!

Don't worry about what people say. Don't talk yourself out of making the change. Don't ignore the scream. Don't beat the donkey. Turn around! You don't have to suffer. You don't have to settle for good enough. You don't have to settle for an average life. You don't have to settle for barely getting by. It's time to make some changes. It's time to pull the reins.

You've tried to turn water to wine and others were drunk. You've tried to use five loaves and two fish to feed the multitudes; you were starved. It's time for you to be filled. Move towards the stream - not away from it. Move forward my friend. Climb the great mountain of love.

You're ready. There's nothing holding you back. You're not being restrained. The donkey laid down under you; but the moment you decided to turn around, she got back up. She's going to carry you to your destiny. My friend, there are great treasures to be found; turn from disaster. Go the other direction and take cover.

You've been struggling for a long time. You're not sure whose voice you're hearing. You're ignoring the urge to do something. Every time you make a move, it seems like you end up right back where you started. You end up right back where you started; because each time you went the wrong way. You've gone the same way many times; try going the other way.

It's a road many will not travel. It's rough at first
- then smooth. You may not be able to see the road
right now; but my friend, there's always another way.
For every right there is a wrong, and every wrong there
is a right. The two go together like the sun and the
moon, light and darkness, night and day.

Don't fight what God's trying to do in your life.
Yes. You are deserving. No. You're not lacking. You
have what it takes. Don't be afraid. You don't know
what the end result will look like. My friend, it's better
than what it looks like now. It's beautiful.

There's more lined up for you. You currently
cannot see it because you're going in the wrong
direction. Make the turn. You're standing on a road in
a flooded valley: trying to keep afloat. Get to high
ground! Yes. Others will be affected by your choice to
change. No worries. I'll be for their good also. Take
some chances. You'll risk some disappointments; but,
it will lead you towards a better life. Consider your way,
pull the reins, and turn back. God's not making a
mistake. He knows exactly what He's doing. Will you
trust Him?

If yes, turn my friend and be exalted. Be delivered to your destiny. Be positioned in the right place. Be surrounded by the right people. Be promoted. Be healed. Be lifted higher! Stay focused on your journey to enlightenment. Stay in love. Enjoy the goodness of God. Dance in His favor. Honor Him, and He'll give you the desires of your heart. My friend, your greater is one turn away.

You have not missed out on your opportunity. It's still sitting right where you left it. *The* Great Spirit will catch you up. He'll put you ahead of where you left off. Yes. He's going to take you further up the road. He's going to supply your needs. He has equipped you. He's going to take you places you never thought you could afford to go. He'll put you in the high position you never thought you'd reach. Yes. He pours out a stream of blessings to flow in your direction. You're going to go from not being able to finish that project: to a job well done.

It's important for you to see yourself arriving at your destiny. I see you walking through the door where peace is waiting for you. I see you making the turn and things begin to shift. I see you walking across that stage with a smile on your face. I'm proud of you. You did it! You made the turn. I see you with not one; but, two children on your hips. I see the woman of your future. You didn't think you'd ever find her; but, she was on the road waiting for you to turn. I see that divorce stopping in the process. I see you being reunited with your child. I see that back pain going away. I see you finally resting upon your bed - because you turned away from stress. I see a promotion. You felt as though you were being unappreciated; that your hard work was going unnoticed. My friend, hard work can never be squeezed into a crack. There will be an appreciation in your honor for a job well done. Do you see what I see?

Friends, if you've decided to make the turn. You are now facing the right direction. You my friend have found the strength; now, move what's blocking your path. You've considered your way, pulled the reins, and turned back; now, move towards what *The* Great Spirit has for you. Make it a plan to succeed. Expect to have what you need. Start rearranging somethings. Start rearranging people in your life. Get rid of dead weight - it will slow you down.

Find someone who's traveled down the road before to be of assistance to you. Stay motivated, alert, and never give up. The straight path usually lies in front of the curve; but, blessed is the man that makes it through the before to see the after. "And thine ears shall hear a word behind thee, saying, this is the way, walk ye in it, when ye turn to the right hand, and when ye turn to the left."

The Great Spirit's About To Take You Higher

Chapter Seven:
Clean Window

If your window is dirty clean it; for clarity of thought, a clear view of what you want, and an unconfused view of what you need. How you view your situation determines the effect it'll have on your life. When looking through a dirty window it's possible to see; however, objects aren't as clear as they should be. The cloudier the window becomes, the harder it is to determine what lies on the other side. When you wipe off the crude; you'll be able to see the big picture. You'll be able to interpret things right. You'll be able to see what's really there - and not just a speck on the glass.

View your circumstances with the right perspective. When you decide to clean your window to let the light in; you're deciding you no longer want to focus on darkness and past hurts. You're deciding to feel the full warmth of the sun: to be able to identify future potential as it approaches. You make the decision you no longer want to see problems; but instead, opportunities.

Often times, we make poor choices when we cannot see things clearly. This is why it's important to clean a dirty window. Maybe like me you're at times impulsive. You tend to move through the decision-making process without thinking things through. You tend to want to move too fast. You want to walk before you learn to crawl. Maybe you let your emotions wrongfully predict the outcome: to create its own conclusion. Clean your window.

Our eyes aren't just the window to the soul. They're also our window to the world. Our minds are like closets; our wardrobe is hung by sight. We get out of it what we put into it. My friend, what we put into it; we usually have to pay for, unless it's a gift. When the mind gets hungry for something *new*, we feed it with perception. If you only feed your mind negativity; it'll

132

have bowel movements full of bad information, and regretful decisions.

This is what happens when you view things from a dirty window. You get bad information. Everything looks worse than it really is. Some things look bigger. Some things look smaller. That purple looks blue, that white is dingy; you can't seem to be able to call a spade a spade - behind that dirty window it looks like a heart. When the batter hits a ball in your direction; you need to know when to move. Otherwise, you'll be sitting there as it shatters the window - giving it no choice but to hit you in the head.

Don't focus on what you don't want - it's a distraction. Focus only on what you want. What we meditate on day and night will become reality in our everyday life. It's possible to send out bad signals. We've been taught from the days of old: "As a man thinketh in his heart so is he."

The more you passionately focus on your circumstances; you become your circumstances. Be aware of the food you put into your mind. When you're faced with a problem: see it as an opportunity - this way you don't attract more problems. My friend, all circumstance: both bad and good, leads to opportunity.

You may not have the greatest view right now. You may not be able to see all the details to paint a better picture. Your circumstance smears up your window. The more you try to wipe the smear away with your hands; it spreads. It's discouraging. It can at times cause you to want to break the window. You don't have to do that. Your window can be cleaned; you just have to use the right product. Spray some positivity on it.

When you start to look at being fired from that job as an opportunity to advance; see that divorce as an opportunity to find true love; see that death making room for birth; see that house burning down as an opportunity to rebuild: you're wiping away negativity. You're cleaning the smears off your window. Some smears are harder to remove than others; but, all can be removed. You don't have to forget the things that have happened to you in your life. It's necessary for you to remember. Spray some positivity on your situation. Allow yourself the opportunity to see things clearly. My friend, attract more light.

You're depressed; feeling down in the dumps because you cannot see beyond the dirt. Maybe you're swimming deep in debt. You have people against your progress. Your future's not looking pretty. You think you'll never overcome sickness. You've become afraid to step outside, because of what you think you see. Do not be discouraged. Spray some positivity on your life. Clean your window.

Stop doubting yourself. Believe you can overcome. Stop squinting your eyes trying to see through a smear. Wipe it away with positive thinking. My friend, I need you to shift your focus and see this. We've all made mistakes and bad decisions in life; but, those mistakes and bad decisions don't define us - they equip us.

What you see is something smaller than what it looks like behind the smear. What you're viewing as a giant in your life, is really a dwarf. Looking through that dirty window is causing you to think everything in your life is going downhill; when it's going up. You cannot see hope on the other side; but she's there. She's waiting for you to change the way you're viewing things. She's waiting for you to wipe the filth off your window. She's waiting to escort you to the house of wisdom. She's waiting to escort you through the door of destiny. Remember my dear friend, as before told: "Hope deferred makes the heart sick..."

If you're to reach your highest potential, you have to first begin to see things clearly. You have to interpret things right. My friend, be willing to change your perspective. Be willing to wipe your window with positivity: no matter how dirty it is. My friend, get rid of the negativity in your life. To do this, let your mind set on the things you want. As I've said before, see yourself there. Don't give your circumstances the control over your life. Control your circumstances. What happens next is up to you. My friend, dig down deep. Get grounded.

If you cannot see *The* Great Spirit working in your life; you're viewing things from a dirty window. You don't see God; but, God's there, *The* Great Spirit is everywhere. It's been said by my Example: "Blessed are the pure in heart: for they shall see God." Could it be the issues of your heart causing you not to see God? Can you imagine that: to be pure enough to look upon the face of *The* Almighty? This means your heart is clean. Your mind is sterilized and unpolluted. It means you have clarity of thought. My friend, look in the right direction for what you desire. View your circumstances from the right angle.

Clean your window. Allow the light of love to come into every inch of your life. Let the desires of your heart be fulfilled. Love is the key to success; anything less is a false start. You can't see this behind a smear. Once you're filled with love you'll have a different view; a different way to understand. What you think you know; you'll realize you never knew. Your view of things will improve. The outcome will be different.

My friends, there's work to be done. No worries. When it's all done: it will be well. You may feel it's impossible to clean your window. You think you cannot accomplish your goals; so you don't set them. Everything looks bad to you. The bowels of your mind is full of bad information it defecates into your life; causing you to interpret things wrong. When good seduces you; often times, you turn it away because you cannot see clearly. You see positive things negatively. My friend, you can change what you see. Your situation can get better. Don't lose faith. Don't stop believing in miracles. Miracles are happening every day.

Be of good cheer my friend. View things with the right perspective. You're looking through a darkened glass; but, you can see hope face to face. Yes. "Hope is there. I've sent her to you. Open your hearts to let her in." Clean your window. Yes. Purify your hearts. Manage your emotions. Stay calm under pressure. Don't hold onto the past. Get rid of dead weight. Yes. Get rid of stress: it causes depression, heart disease, and obesity. Don't drag the issues of your past into your present. Let it go. Yes. Let it go. Grab hold of your purpose.

Stop reliving those events over and over again through others. The person you're projecting to is not you. How can you protect them when you can't see them? You have to be able to watch them from a clean window: to know, to understand, to trust, to love - to see them coming a mile away. My friend, everything is not dirty. Everyone is not dirty. Your window is dirty. Wipe the crude off your window. Spray some positivity on it. Wipe it away.

Seeing things clearly is when you can separate your wants from your needs; and know the difference between the two. You see things clearly when you're able to stop worrying about the probabilities; and start believing in the opportunities. You'll see things clearly after you remove the scribbled *what if* from your view.

Your attitude should be: "I may not be where I want to be right now; but, I'm going to get there. I know God's taking me to a new level in my life. I may not be able to see what I need right now; but, I know it's there. I may not be able to see her; but, I believe Hope is waiting for me." My friend, when your thoughts turn negative; shift your attention to positive things. Be grateful for what you have.

Your window is clean; but it's storming outside. Your window is clean; but, you can't see due to the fog. Someone is standing in the way of your view. Hold your head up high my love. Endure. The storm will be over soon. Take this time to clean house. Take this time to rest and relax. Take this time to study and prepare. *The* Great Spirit's tending to your garden. He's watering the seeds you've planted.

Wipe the tears from your eyes my love. God will move the fog away quickly when it's done. Your season is about to change. Preparations are being made. You're about to see more than you were able to see before. You're about to notice more than you were able to notice before.

Grab hold to good emotions my love. Ask that person to move out of your way. Some people don't know they're in the way. Let them know. My mama use to say, "Your ass aint made of glass Ne'kka. Stop standing in front of the TV." You know what I did? I moved. I didn't know I was in the way. I had to be told. Tell them. If you tell them and they refuse to move, you move. That's the good thing about your window: you carry it with you wherever you go.

Have no worries about your future my love. There's a blessing poured over you. *The* Great Spirit will: "Give you the dew of heaven, the fatness of the earth, and an abundance of more than enough."

I wonder how many of you are not seeing things clearly because your eyes are closed. Open them. You've been focused on darkness long enough. It's time for you to focus on the light. It's time for you to see the truth. I know you've been wounded to the core; cut down through the white meat. I know you're trying to protect yourself. Many of you don't want to see because you don't want to know. My friend, has it been easy to not know? If you're anything like me, the answer to the question is no. No matter how hard you try not to see it; the light still shines in the darkness. *The* Great Spirit's chosen you to do a work for Him. He chose you. You cannot run from that. You can try; but, believe me I wouldn't.

Your window is spotless. God's cleared the way for you. Open your eyes to see it. Stop telling yourself: "Well, if I try to fit in; things will get better. *John Doe* loves me. *Sally Cool Cat* is my friend. What if I fail? What if I fall alone and there's no one there to lift me up?" My love, "*The* Great Spirit has given His Angels charge over you: to keep you in all your ways." Open your eyes. See the beauty in you. You are what you seek my friend - enough.

It's not ok to consume your cleaning products; but in this case, you need to drink some positivity. Let it get deep down in your spirit. Start sparkling from the inside out. I'm encouraging you to do so. Positivity is an all-purpose cleaner. It can clean out the bowels of your mind; the sickness of your body, and remove the bandits from your heart. It causes the blood to flow properly from the top of your head to the bottom of your feet. It takes the swelling down and removes the color from the bruise. It allows you to focus. My friend, the dreams and desires placed in your heart will soon enough be your reality. When you take a sip of positivity; you take a sip of faith. You should have enough faith inside of you; that it fills your belly, then becomes like vomit out of your mouth.

Enough faith to tell somebody: "This is where I am; but, this is not my destiny. *The* Great Spirit has something bigger and better for me. It may not look like it. It may not sound like it. But I know I'm equipped. I have what I need. I know God will provide. I know He'll make a way out of no way. I have the confidence to become. I have the talent to become. No obstacle can stand in my path and be victorious over me. I will run through and leap over. I will not bow down. I will not crawl under."

Yes. You should have enough faith to claim your package before it arrives. My friend, take a sip of positivity and go tell somebody: "My blessing is on the way. It has my name on it. I'll get what belongs to me. My window was dirty; but now, it's clean. I once was blind; but now, I see. I see *The* Deliverer. I see my Healing. I see Love. I see Hope waiting for me."

My friend, don't let your house go unattended - clean every day. Dirt particles are naturally attracted to your light. Don't let them build up on your window. It can be challenging to remove them once they've settled. They'll feed your mind doubts, cover up truth, and hide hope. They'll constantly deceive you with thoughts of failure. They'll feed your mind so much negativity; it'll have bowel movements such as: "You'll never amount to anything. You don't have what it takes. It'll never happen for you. You won't ever find what you're looking for. You should always expect the worst."

They'll try to convince you to need what you don't need. Don't allow them to block your view of the sun. See things clearly. Clean your window. Yes. See things for what they are, and not what they appear to be. We're to walk by faith and not by sight; so that when the enemy tries' to block our view of Hope; we know she's there.

There was a time I lost my mind. I was called many names, and given labels of all kinds of crazy. So much so, that I began to believe it. So much so, that I peered through a dirty window and could not see my reflection. I could no longer see *The* Great Spirit smiling back at me. I couldn't remember what the real me looked like. I couldn't remember my purpose. I couldn't focus on good. I could only feel hurt. I could only remember pain accompanied by resentment.

Yes. I was surrounded by darkness. I wanted to give into it. I wanted to just throw in the towel. I wanted to take my own life. Not because of some vain thing. No. I felt I'd lost my one true love. I thought God had left me. I thought He turned me over to a reprobate mind. I felt naked and ashamed. I felt abandoned and alone.

Ever feel like this before? Ever get so overwhelmed you want to throw in the towel? Ever lose sight of hope? My friend, I knew my window was dirty the moment I started to believe: what God promised me was impossible to obtain. I knew I wasn't seeing things clearly when I started allowing others to dictate my future.

Truth be told, *The* Great Spirit never left me. He was there all along. I couldn't see Him because my window was full of crude. Not just my crude either. I let other people wipe their nasty sticky hands all over my window. I had to remember what God told me before I started the journey. I had to remember the promises He made. I had to remember all the things He's brought me through. I had to trust Him. I only had a small bucket of faith; but, I knew it was enough to get the job done. I scrubbed the negativity away. The light is bursting through the darkness. My friends, I see Hope.

If your life's stressful, dark, and depressing; try cleaning your window. Stop trying to see behind the smear of that addiction. Wipe away bad habits. You don't need those drugs. You don't need that gang. You don't need that abusive and neglectful relationship.

What you're going through now is just a speck on your window. That divorce is a speck on your window. That job layoff is a speck on your window. That foreclosure notice is a speck on your window. That repossession is a speck on your window. Wipe it away with positivity. Declare no matter how bad things look; there's hope. See yourself overcoming. Speak over yourself. My friend, breathe life into your desires.

Yes. Wipe off the lies telling you: "Things are never going to get better." The lies telling you, "It's too late because you've made too many mistakes." Wipe away the thought of giving up. Press on. The fire inside you was lit to be seen. It was lit so others could find their way home through dark times. It was lit to guide the way. Clean your window. Let your light be seen brightly shining in the distance.

If you feel you cannot remove all the spots yourself, ask for help. Help is always available when you need it; you just have to remember to ask for it. I don't want you to go through life feeling defeated. I declare, your ship shall sail to victory with *The* Great Spirit as your captain. Clean your window. Enjoy the journey. My friend, clean your window. Be restored to good health, obtain wisdom, and experience the favor of God. My love, clean your window. See the opportunity. Yes. Clean your window. Hope is waiting for you.

See It For What It Is; A Spot on Your Window.

Chapter Eight:
Act Brand New

I was speaking with my friend Nicole about some changes to be made in my life. We've known each other since high school. We've encouraged one another since to do work right with God. That day, maybe she noticed a different tone in my voice. One that was not familiar to her. So she responded, "Don't act brand new with me." I meditated on those words as she continued to speak.

I'd heard the saying before; but to me, it made no sense at all. I thought: *why should I not act brand new? I'm not the same as I once was. My flesh maybe familiar; but on the inside I'm new. I'm whole. I'm refreshed, reconditioned, and restored by the hands of God.*

Friends, when you're born again in the Spirit of Love, you become a new creation. The old you passes away and should be laid to rest. Therefore, you should act brand new. Remember our teachings from the days of old: "No man putteth a piece of new cloth unto an old garment, for that which is put in to fill it up taketh from the garment, and the rent is made worse. Neither do men put new wine into old bottles: else the bottles break, and the wine runneth out, and the bottles perish: but they put new wine into new bottles, and both are preserved."

For years, I struggled with laying old habits to rest. I worried about the friends I'd lose. I worried about my reputation. I worried about not being equipped and enough. I was worrying about the wrong things.

When you're made brand new, it's like being born again. Many make the journey; but, only a few find the egg to make it through. You'll have to spend some time in the womb - this is necessary for transformation. Like the caterpillar that eats up the farmer's garden then draws into himself to become a butterfly: to pollinate the flowers and the trees of the world - that they may bear fruit. You don't have to do much at this time. Wait and let nature take its course. You're nestled and protected in the belly of *The* Great Spirit. Trust Him. He'll provide your needs. Don't be dismayed when you feel the change approaching. It's your time for growth. It's your time of rest. It's the time to prepare for what's to come.

In the womb you may feel like your life is at a standstill. You may begin to evaluate your surroundings. You may begin to consider your dealings with others. You may not be able to see or understand your progress. Will you kick against the walls of God? Will you sit quietly in His womb smiling and sucking your thumb? Will you cry when the midwife smacks your bottom? Will you laugh?

When you're delivered into righteousness, you gaze into the eyes of love. Friends, this is when you're brand new. Your past is like a dream. You'll have to start learning the things you thought you knew all over again. You'll have to learn to open your eyes, hold your head up, crawl, and walk. You'll have to learn how to communicate with others. You'll have to learn how to share with another. You'll have to learn how to observe, read, and make good decisions. Don't be discouraged if you fall the first time you try to walk upright. Keep trying my friend. One day you'll run and not get weary.

It's important for us to act brand new. How can we live a new life trying to live the old life? This only creates confusion. Think about when you're hired to do a job: you have to dress the part, look the part, talk the part, and oftentimes live the part. Sometimes, you have to spend a lot of money to go to school a lot of years - to ensure you play the part right.

My friend, you're hanging out late at night on the street corner; but, that's not the life chosen for you. You don't have to settle for constantly having to look over your shoulder. You don't have to feel ashamed of wanting to be different. You don't have to feel ashamed of wanting to act brand new. You don't have to feel ashamed of making the choice to see with lights on. You have the choice to become greater. My friend, they said you were "Never going to be nothing:" don't mean it's true.

There's a new life waiting for you. When you begin to act brand new; *The* Great Spirit's going to take you to a "perfect place." I don't know who you are. I don't know where you live. But my friend, one day, I'll know your name. I'll look upon your face and be in awe of your talent. Your light will shine so bright - it will be seen around the world.

Understand my dear friend, this is not an easy task; however, it's one of foreseen victory. Surround yourself with people whose words give birth to good things. Learn of their ways. Hear their instructions. Don't let your feet run before you to do work that's not good. Yes. Some people will turn and walk out of your life. Let them go. Yes. You'll find it hard for a moment to make ends meet. No worries. God will provide. You may be dirty, lying down in your own vomit. No worries. God will clean you up. Yes. You will be lied on. You will be talked about. No worries. "Time will tell."

My dear chosen ones, arise! Get up and take your place. Shed the old you. Take off the mask and become true to who you've been called to be. Tell the truth placed on your heart. This truth is called Love. Yes. Sugar in water does taste sweet; but, too much sugar is not good for you. This is what I mean using simple words: you don't have to conform to this world.

151

We're from a different place - a place where water is healing nectar. We step in weak; but my friend, we come out strong and powerful. Do you understand? Do you understand that we have the power to change the world? That we have a choice to stand or sit? That we no longer have to wear that hot sweaty mess of a mask anymore? Lights of the world, shine, and shine bright.

In order to act brand new, we have to get rid of old things. We have to get rid of old attitudes that no longer serve our purpose. We have to stop thinking about what we can't do, and start believing in what we can do. We have to walk away from somethings: to move towards somethings. We have to let some people go. We have to let some thoughts dissolve. We have to speak as though it is so. We have to live our lives according to that in which we're called.

Yes. Some who act brand new are raggedy inside. They play the role. They've become proficient in the language; however, they lack the value of truth for gain. Like wolves in sheep's clothing, they've confused nations - false prophets whose hearts are made of stone. My friend, I'm telling you this so you're aware: the enemy knows how to smile in your face while holding the knife to your back. Be of good cheer my dears, and do not fear: as a mother protects a child, *The* Great Spirit protects you even more.

I was verbally abused. For a long time, I didn't understand why. I believed I was fat and ugly. I began to believe everything I once known beyond a shadow of doubt to be true: was hallucination or illusion. I believed I wasn't good enough - that I didn't have what was necessary. I tried to look past it; but the more and more I heard it, the more it became the reality of my life. I started to feel helpless, weak, lost: confused about my identity. I was being forced to give up my last bit of hope. Fear of failure kicked in: *What if they're right? What if God didn't tell me to do any of this at all? What if I'm who they say I am? What if this is all God has for me?*

My friend, I was ready to wave the white flag. I was ready to give up. Then I heard *The* Great Spirit, "Who do I say that you are? What do I say you can do? Is it my habit to treat you this way? Trust me. Follow me. It is well my daughter... It is done my daughter..." I tell you the truth my friend, I'm not confident holding this cup; but, I'd rather drink to fill my thirst, then to not drink and die full of void.

I heard a pastor of a church ask a question one Sunday: "Have you ever heard the saying, sticks and stones may break my bones; but words will never hurt me? That's a lie. Sticks and stones may hurt for days, weeks, maybe even months, but words can hurt someone for decades. Words can either make a person or break a person." I've found this to be true.

Some people in your life are comfortable with the way you are. My friend, they don't want things to change. They'll say hurtful mean things to make you feel low. They know when you feel good about yourself; you feel good about your future. They know when you fly high on life; you see more than just the ground. Some fear they'll be forced to respect you. Others fear you'll walk away. That late-night *booty call* knows when you begin to act brand new; you're going to want more. You're going to want commitment. Some of you will say in your Ciara voice, "No not my goodies," and others will sound more like Beyoncé, "If you liked it, then you should have put a ring on it." My friend, this is the type of change that *booty call* wants to avoid.

154

Maybe your spouse is afraid of change; wanting to rule over you rather than to reign beside you. My friend, this isn't about you at all. This is about something they're afraid to face within themselves; baggage from their past they're refusing to unpack: out of fear something would be stolen from them. Sometimes, they don't want to grow old. They cling to their youth.

This can make it hard for you to change. This person knows how to entice you. They know how to distract you. What do you do? How can you act brand new? How can you act brand new when your loved ones choose to remain where they are? My friend, do what it is you've been called to do. Be an example. Spend your time in spirit. Do what you can do, and leave the rest for God. If it's meant to be, it will be. *The Great Spirit has this amazing way of turning chaos to order. Get out of His way. Will you trust Him?

My friend, you're being bullied because to others who cannot see clearly, you seem different in some way. You seem like an easy target; another step to get them to where they want to be. You rationalize their behavior. You want a friend so bad; you're willing to let them treat you any way they want. Some of you fight back: others shut down. You cry out; but you feel as though no one hears you. I hear you. I feel your pain. I know your suffering. Keep pressing on my friend. The storm will be over soon. The sun is there my love. It's shining behind the clouds. Find peace within yourself. I need you to survive.

When you begin to act brand new, some people in your life are going to be hungry and have to eat their own words. They'll be accountable for every wicked thing. We can pray for them; but in this case, we will not be able to save them - they've been warned. I know what it looks like: It looks like they treat you like dirt, and God blesses them for throwing mess on you. My friend, I'm going to tell you what He told me, "I'm going to take them all the way up, but they will fall back down. Their foot shall slip in due time: for the day of their calamity is at hand, and the things that shall come upon them make haste."

My friend, don't worry about what your situation looks like; believe in what *The* Great Spirit says your future will be like. He'll bring order to your house – even if it means moving some people out. He sees how your boss is treating you. Get out of His way. Trust Him. My friend, place your worries in Gods care. Cast your cares on Him. Remember, "All things work together for good to them that love God, to them who are the called according to His purpose." Trust him.

Acting brand new is not the same as becoming better than anyone else. It's not surrounding yourself with a bunch of stuff. It's not about keeping up with *the Joneses*. It's about becoming the best you; but understanding similarities of apples and oranges. Yes. Both are fruit and have their time to ripen. My friend, do what you know in your heart to be right out of love - no matter what.

If you've pressed against the soil; if you've sprouted: then act like things have taken root in your life. If you've been lathered up – cleansed; don't go rolling around in the mud with pigs. You can pet them, feed them, and talk to them; but, you don't have to lay down in their mess. If you've established constant flow; stop acting like you're dying of thirst. Stop acting like *The* Great Spirit hasn't been at work in your life. My friend, start acting like what you are: blessed.

You have let go of the hot pot; now, start acting like your hands are free. Get to work. Act like you've forgiven the person you claim to forgive. Don't go around digging up old bones, rolling your eyes, and smacking your lips. If you've pulled the reins; if you've change course, you don't have to keep going in circles. Move forward. Things have already turned around for you. If your window was dirty, and you've cleaned it; start acting like you can see hope on the other side. Rejoice!

The Great Spirit doesn't do things halfway. He didn't clean you up to have you sitting there looking pretty. He has work for you to do. You're about to start a new job in righteousness. You're going to have to dress right for this job. No. Your worldly wardrobe won't do. I don't care how much it cost. You're going to have to put on the whole armor of God. Never take it off.

If feel you can do this job without God; when you feel you've made it as far as you have alone; take a moment to remember where you came from. Remember where He picked you up from. Remember where He turned you around. Remember: how you were sinking;

and He placed your feet on solid ground. Remember when you were a broken mess and He made you whole. When He performed miracles in spite of what the doctor said; In spite of what mommy and daddy did; In spite of where your enemies were standing: in spite of the weapons formed against you.

No. Don't get high and mighty standing on fowl and dung. My friend, remember where you came from. Remember what it was like to be treated as a rug to be walked all over. Remember what it felt like to be pushed down - beat down. Remember: so you store up compassion for others. Without this my friends, you'd be wolves in sheep's clothing: not new at all - just well costumed.

How you act in your normal day to day lives will help determine your future. I'm not talking about acting like *when Sunday comes saints*. I'm talking about seven days a week; 365 days out of a year: commitment, to doing the best you can possibly do; while being the best you can possibly be. If you continue to go through life acting like you're a failure; acting like you're not good enough; comparing your success to the success of others; thinking it's all too much for you to handle; you'll stop yourself from getting the best God has for you. If you continue to go through life talking bad about yourself; everyday reminding yourself of a lie you've created - or been told; the lie that tells you: "you can't" or, "you'll never;" you'll stop yourself from getting the best God has for you. My friend, don't act defeated. You're the victor. Start acting like it.

Stop walking around like an old pair of shoes: flapping with a bad attitude, having no faith and falling apart. Ever wear a pair of shoes to the point they'd fall apart? To the point that piece by piece, bit by bit, crusted, rusted, and busted? I have. When I was younger, we use to say shoes talked when the outer sole separated from the rest of the shoe. It created a flap that resembled a mouth. Opening and closing with each step. Those old shoes would flap so much; just talk- talk -talk, disturbing the peace, they tell you: "It's time to get a new pair of shoes."

In this case: all that complaining, griping, moaning and groaning; is telling you it's time to act brand new. It's time to start making some changes. How long have you been complaining about that same problem? How long have you been flapping about those same issues? It's time to find the solution. It's time to start acting brand new in the spirit. It's time to start believing brand new in the spirit. It's time to start thinking brand new in the spirit. Yes. Start acting like it's done.

Remember what it felt like when you got that new pair of shoes? How they allowed you the opportunity to walk right? How they helped you run fast and jump high? How it helped to boost your confidence to walk into a room with your head up? This is what it's like to be new in spirit.

My friend, you shouldn't be bothered by the wind blowing the waves; you're being carried to your destination in the hands of God. There's nothing anyone can say about you that would convince Him not to love you. You are a mark on the drawing - you matter. Without you the drawing would be incomplete. Yes. You have a position. You have a purpose. Some of us are drawn with color and definition; some of us are drawn with faint lines; but, we're all a part of the big picture. Do you understand?

I understand what my friend heard in my voice that day. She was hearing me say: *I put it all in the hands of The Great Spirit. I'm not going to worry about it. I'm not going to keep talking about it - it's done.* Nothing against her; but as women, we love to sit on the phone with our girlfriends complaining. We complain about the people at work, talk about our *no good mates*; and magnify our problems. I've been guilty of this. These conversations end or begin in gossip. I don't have time for that. I don't have time to complain.

My friend, it's dangerous to complain when you've prayed for the results you want. You might magnify your problems so much; people begin to pray against the very thing you've been praying for. That's why it's important to act like it's done.

I wanted to change when I realized I was distracted by vanity, control, and lust. This is when I started acting brand new. This was the only way for me to do what it is I'm called to do. I tried all other ways. Believe me when I tell you; I tried to get away from it. But my friend, I just began to fall apart like that old pair of shoes. I know no other way.

My friend, if you're beginning to fall apart; if pieces of you are being left behind: it's time to purchase newness in yourself. It's time to get rid of self-doubt,

162

pride, selfishness, envy, and anything that doesn't burn fire under the cause. Yes. If it's snuffing out your flame; get rid of it.

You don't need money. This newness is free to both the poor and the rich. All you need is a willingness to do what's necessary to claim reward. My friend, submit to the will of *The* Great Spirit. Walk in the light of Love. Live in the light of Love. Work in the light of Love. Play in the light of Love. Endure in the light of Love. Everything you do: let it be in love.

When you become new; when you start acting new; take notice of your thoughts. You'll be tempted to lust after the old you. You'll be tempted to put the mask back on. Don't do it. There was a reason you felt the need to take it off in the first place. Sure, thoughts may come to you like: "What was I thinking? I can't change. This is too hard. I'm tired. Why can't I just be like everyone else? Why can't I do what they do? Why can't I just be normal?"

My Friend, you've been set apart because there's a calling placed on your life. You had to put away the old you. Focus on the new you. Be "renewed in knowledge after the image of Him that created you."

Who said you were different? Who told you you're not normal? Do you know who you truly are? Let me tell you as it has been told to us before: "Ye are a chosen generation, a royal priesthood, an holy nation, a peculiar people; that ye should shew forth the praises of Him who hath called you out of darkness into His marvelous light: which in time past were not a people, but are now the people of God: which had not obtained mercy, but now have obtained mercy." My friend, you had to shed old skin to grow larger in the grace of God.

I encourage you to take inventory of what you possess within yourself. You shouldn't be carrying some of the same things you were carrying before. What caused your old vessel to sink; shouldn't be onboard your new vessel: lessen you want to suffer the same fate. When you notice something that doesn't belong: get rid of it. Start by declaring you're a new creation. Yes. Old things have passed away - all things are made new. Therefore, that addiction doesn't belong to you. That heartache doesn't belong to you. That depression doesn't belong to you. That anger doesn't belong to you. No. God says, "Vengeance is mine."

Lights of the world, faith belongs to you. Yes. Joy belongs to you. Peace belongs to you. The victory is yours; and concerning wisdom, knowledge, and understanding: it's readily available for use. Remember this when you struggle to stay afloat.

Don't keep going through life settling for the worst; when you can have the best. You don't have to keep playing that same old role. *The* Great Spirit's molding you like clay. Yes. He's shaping and defining your life. He'll place you in the fire for a time to strengthen you. No worries my friend. You'll come out a new creation. Not the type of creation He'd want to hide in a chest. No. He's going to place you up high: for all to see. You have value. *The* Great Spirit will protect you. He'll keep you safe. My friend, He'll use you on occasion. Yes. He'll fill your void with His nectar: others will drink from you. If you fall and break; He'll be right there to pick up the pieces. Yes. Be of good cheer my friend: God will repair your soul.

Act Like It's Done

The hope of a secure and livable

world lies with disciplined nonconformists

who are dedicated to justice, peace

and brotherhood

Martin Luther King, Jr.

Chapter Nine:
Carried by Waves

Life is a constant cycle - it happens. I often find myself in situations out of my control. It doesn't matter how hard I try, how hard I pray, or how hard I fight : the end results are the same. We all experience situation and circumstance. Situations that seem impossible to overcome; Circumstance that makes it easy to become bitter and discouraged: What do you do? Nothing.

You surrender. You allow the waves that are only stilled by the hands of God to carry you. You may be tossed to and fro, banged up against some rocks, or caught in the net; however, it's all necessary for your arrival. Yes. Loss, failure, sickness, old age, decay, pain, and death; are all necessary waves.

You may not understand why things are happening to you; you may feel helpless and for a time lost. Your life may seem meaningless. You'll at some point breakdown and become victim to disorder. You may feel like God has abandoned you. You may feel like He doesn't exist. Your faith is sure to be tested; and your strength discovered inadequate. You may try to swim your way out: only to find that you end up you right back where you started. If you trust in *The* Great Spirit my friend; you'll wash up on fertile land to become treasure.

You must not swim against the current; it's a waste of time and energy. The most beneficial thing you can do is surrender. Surrender to the constant change in your life. Swim parallel to it. Some things you can fight against and win; but, you cannot win against the waves of God in your life. They're there to carry you to your destiny.

Like a surfer, learn how to flow with the waves instead of trying to fight against them. Let the waves carry you to where your destiny awaits. You have the option to go in either direction without there being a right or a wrong way. My friend, to get there you must flow. Don't worry about not being able to swim. Surrender; and you'll become a part of the waves with purpose: instead of a lost foreign object seemingly without hope.

My friend, you're going to wash up where God's explored before. He's secured the outcome to work in your favor. You're having experiences beneficial for the outcome. You may not have the understanding right now; you may not be able to connect the dots; but, you don't need to worry precious jewel.

The waves are washing up the right people in your life and drifting the wrong people away. They're washing up opportunities. They're forming firm places for you to stand. Yes. They're banging you up against the rocks so you'll get a good break. You're caught in the net for your protection. Do you not see the shark with its mouth open? He will not dare go near the net. But if he's brave, bold, and full of enough courage; he'll then be caught up to set you free.

You've experienced loss. Maybe it was a house, car, job, child, spouse, or even your mind. It's easy to become bitter. It's easy to give into the seduction of negativity. It's easy to think: "My life is over. There's no hope for me. Nothing will ever change. I'm cursed. I have bad karma." You may find yourself depressed, impatient, frustrated, and stressed. So much so, you make yourself sick. Surrender.

My love, you will not be able to solve the problems in your life until you submit to the waves. Just Be. This is all you have to do to become. God knows where you are; He put you there. Everything about you is written in the book of life. It's been said, "The very hairs of your head are all numbered." Every setback is to propel you forward. God's in control. He knows what He's doing. It's for your good. The only thing you have control of now is the choice to act or react. Surrender to the will of God. Become. Arrive on time. You'll wash up beautifully and wonderfully made; victorious, and fulfilled.

You may find yourself often complaining about many occurrences in life. Constantly thinking about what you *coulda, shoulda, woulda* done but didn't do.

Actually thinking you had control over the outcome. Instead of looking in the mirror to see your flaws; or because you cannot explain it; you'll find someone or something to blame. This is how you fight against the waves. What's done is done. You cannot change it no matter how hard you try. Time simply will not allow it. My friend, keep flowing - no matter what.

Things may rub up against you. You may flow into some mess. Others may get in the way. You may be covered by a wave that carries you so far under to the point you believe; you'll never be able to breathe again. I promise you children of *The* Most High, when you surrender; you'll float back to the top.

Sometimes there's nothing you can do to prevent the outcome. That's why the song goes to say, "After you've done all you can, you just stand." Surrender and let God do the rest. Yes. Let go and let God. If you stay in faith and be present in the moment; you'll see God at work in your life. You'll see *The* Great Spirit commanding the wind and calming the seas.

It may take a while for you to see in totality. Understand some, not all things can happen overnight. That pain you feel takes time to dissolve. I know it hurts. I know what it feels like to be helpless and partly ashamed: to feel like you've done something wrong; to want to crawl under a rock and just die. I've been there before.

The day I found out I was pregnant with my first child was the happiest day of my life. I was so happy I couldn't stop crying. When I told the father he wasn't happy at all. He went into a rage, "I didn't want any children; especially, not with you. It's a mistake." The insults kept coming. I was in complete shock. I couldn't believe what I was hearing. We'd been together for almost four years. If you'd witnessed what I had to stomach that day; you would've thought my conception was the result of a one night stand. He broke up with me the same day: told me all about his plans to leave me. He didn't leave. Although there were times I wished he would.

At 20 weeks, I informed my doctor of sharp pains. Without giving me an ultrasound, she said, "It's just some pelvic rounding; you'll be okay." I knew something was wrong. Two weeks into my pregnancy I had a dream my baby was dead. I placed her in a suitcase and sat her up high on a shelf. I didn't close the lid: to protect her from the *demons* or *vampires* I was fighting in my dream. When I went back to check on her she was gone. I continued to fight. Suddenly, in the midst of the battle, a little girl appeared between me and my enemies. It was my daughter. She exploded into a white light; destroying all who stood against me.

I didn't understand what my dream meant at the time. I didn't even know I was having a girl. I've been promised a son. Sure enough, December 30, 2014, I gave birth to a beautiful baby girl. What would've been the happiest day of my life was the saddest. She was early; and because she was only twenty one weeks: for an hour I watched her die in my arms.

Yes. I went into labor at 3:00 am on December 29th. I arrived at Tri-city hospital at 3:30 am. The contractions were not showing up on the machines; however, I was definitely feeling something. After multiple ultrasounds my doctor discovered: I was in labor and dilated a centimeter.

I was transferred to Mary Birch for a cervical cerclage. I arrived there at 10:00 am. After arriving to my room numbered 316; I sat there with no worries: full of hope. I watched the clock. Wondering when the surgery was going to start. Soon after, the doctor called to inform: they'd postponed my surgery until 3:00 pm. I was baffled.

The doctor arrived at 2:30 pm to perform an ultrasound. When she did, my whole world crashed and burned. I was dilated to 4 centimeters. There was nothing they could do to stop premature labor. I was still hopeful. Even the baby's father went into a raging babble, "Why would they care flight you here; make you wait all this time: only to tell you there's nothing they can do? If they would have done something when you got here we wouldn't be having this problem now." He was upset; but, he took the words right out of my mouth. It was their fault my baby was going to die. I really believed this.

1:00 am: I was hungry, tired, and confused. The moment I closed my eyes, the bearer of bad news arrived. He took every bit of hope I had left away from me. Every positive thing I'd say, this man would come back at me with double negatives. My contractions were seemingly slowing down. When he brought his negative energy in, they quickly sped back up.

After he gave me all the statistics and told me they wouldn't do anything for my baby. He refused to answer my questions; cutting me off at every turn. I asked him to leave: he wouldn't leave. I screamed at the top of my lungs. Finally, he got it. But by then it was too late. I was given an epidural, Ambien, and pumped with some form of antibiotic. I threw up. *Nurse, I think my water broke.* No. It was not my water. At 3:14 am, I gave birth to Sky Keylianna Denier.

I was in a stage of disbelief. I didn't even cry. I still had hope. I prayed: *God I need a miracle.* Begged: *God please. Please save my baby.* I knew *The* Great Spirit could do it. I knew He could do that which was impossible to man. I believed He was going to make them eat their scientific words. No. He did nothing: at least that's what I believed at the time.

The baby's father asked me what the number 316 stood for. I couldn't think straight; but it finally came to me: *It's a scripture, "For God so loved the world that He gave His only begotten son, that whosoever believe in Him shall not perish but have everlasting life.*

Hours later, when moved into a different room; I finally broke down in tears: *Sky, you could've waited.*

My heart stopped. I was so hurt. *Nobody's faith had been stronger than my faith.* I felt betrayed. I'd done everything God asked me to do; but, He continued to make me suffer.

What's the point of me sharing this story with you? I want you to know that I know the pain you're feeling right now. I know the magnitude of resentment; the thought of betrayal. I know what it feels like to be crushed by a wave. Wanting to just drown in sorrows; shut down, and give up on it all.

I received a message a couple days later from spirit: "Somethings you have no control over." The message opened my eyes to the waves in my life. Huh. They were all causing me to move forward.

I realize there's nothing I could do to get myself out of the deep: when God has put me there. My worries began to fade away in the distance. I acquired understanding from the words of the preacher, "Vanity of vanities, all is vanity." I surrender. I'm going to float and flow on the waves in my life.

Waves, are the forward movement of the ocean's water due to the alternating of water particles. This is done by way of friction with the wind. Get this:

friction can mean hostility, conflict, tension, strife, disagreement, roughness, or resistance. My friend, *The Great Spirit's* moving things around to work in your favor. He's using the waves in your life to shift the atmosphere.

We don't know what He knows. We cannot see in our form what He sees. My friend, He's working it out. Remember what I've said before: affliction will divide a man for the purpose of increase; it's best to be as the bush at this time - burnt but not consumed.

There are waves meant to wake you up from sleep. Waves that'll get you going towards the path of enlightenment. Waves caused by your own actions. Waves to put you back on course, and waves to lift you up higher. Nothing you're going through is free labor. What you've spent; you're going to get double that. What you've sacrificed is going to come back to you in time. Every injustice you had to endure was a step closer to your destiny. Heartache and pain will dissolve; love and joy will take their place. My friend, you're being seasoned, and in your season, not even the strongest winds could knock you down. You'll surf the waves.

You may not be able to see past the obstacle at this time. Maybe you're starting to feel emotionally or spiritually dehydrated. Maybe you're bitter or discouraged. Asking yourself: "What's the point of living?" Feeling like you're not getting anywhere. You can't see land in the distance. It's there. Surrender. Stop swimming against the waves. Let the waves carry you.

In time, you'll realize everything has happened for a reason. Every wave has created the necessary changes of your life. God's not out to get you. He doesn't hate you. He hasn't abandoned you. He loves you. He'll settle for nothing less than the best beneficial outcome for you.

When you surrender, there'll be less salt in your eyes. You'll see *The* Great Spirit positioning you in His favor. Yes. You'll see the land in the distance. You no longer have to fight. If they want to go: let them go. You're your responsibility. You cannot control their actions. If people want to swim with the sharks: let them. Maybe they need to be bitten to recognize the danger. Pray for them - let the waves carry you.

My friend, surrender to that hurt. Surrender to that disappointment. Surrender to those unfair situations. Surrender to those setbacks. Surrender to what people say about you. Yes. Let time tell. Surrender to guilt. Surrender to shame. No. Start surfing the waves. Don't let them keep you down. Rise above it all. Don't drown in self-pity.

Those waves in your life are thrusting you forward to land flowing with milk and honey. You'll be found as treasure. You'll have a fresh start – a new beginning. You can build on a solid foundation. Yes. You don't have to worry. You're valued more than rubies.

My friend, you're the treasure you seek. You just haven't taken the time to find you yet. Take the time to find you. Know who you are. Know your worth. What treasure is found to be worthless?

My love, all the things you've endured have increased your value. Maybe you or someone you love was diagnosed with an illness. Maybe you lost everything in disaster. Maybe your spouse or significant other ran out on you. Your business failed. You got fired from your job. You're falsely accused. You were beaten. You were raped. Something was taken from you. You were cast out. My friends, these are all waves. They've happened for a reason. "It's for good and not evil, to give you a future and a hope." I know it seems cruel and unfair; nevertheless, there's land in the distance.

You got pregnant at an early age: that child is supposed to grow up to make a difference in this world. You flunked out of college: there's something else you need to be doing - you're equipped. You lost "everything:" you need to know what it feels like to seemingly have nothing - you'll get it back. Do the right thing. Those people abandoned you: they were not good for you in the first place. My friend, learn how to surf the waves.

When you swim against the waves you burn yourself out. You waste needed energy. You'll find yourself struggling to rise above it all. You'll find yourself struggling to keep afloat. Anxiety and depression will creep in like a thief in the night, and steal away hope. Yes. They'll take all you value and leave you with a mess of confusion.

Carried by Waves

My friend, stop trying to take matters into your own hands. Stop trying to control the outcome - let it come. You don't have the power to still the water. You don't have the power to calm the seas. No. You do not have the power to command the wind. I know you feel stranded in life; but if you don't surrender to the waves: you'll be moved by crisis at every turn.

I've witnessed young men trying to take matters into their own hands by selling drugs. Young women: looking for love in all the wrong places, settling for less than their worth, prostituting their bodies for pennies and to lick pipes. You're only creating unnecessary waves in your life. You're trying to get to shore before your time. *The* Great Spirit will cause rip currents to put you back in place. Maybe it's by way of imprisonment, unplanned pregnancy, witness to a murder, or coming face to face with death. I beseech you my love, surrender. My friend, you've gotten yourself into some hot water - it burns. Your outlook should be: "God I know you'll never put more on me than I can bear. I may not see what you're doing; but, I know you're doing something for my good. I surrender all. I'm going to wait on you. I'm going to trust you!"

Hope To A Friend Sunrise

Things may not look good right now. It seems like there's no hope for your future. But God's stilling the waters. You're going to wash up on fertile land. You are treasure to be found. *The* Great Spirit has arranged your new beginning. There's land in the distance. Build on good emotions. Wash up strong, victorious, and shining in glory.

My friend, you're facing some waves that seem impossible to ride. You fear they'll crush your dreams and drown your hopes. You feel helpless, stranded, and lost; outnumbered: feeling weak and wounded by circumstance. So much so, you feel you won't survive. You feel you don't have a chance. If you have nothing my friend, have faith. Surrender where you are and be present in that moment. Flow and let the waves carry you to your destiny.

Surf the waves. You will rise above it all. Surrender to the will of God. Yes. Let what will be - be. Waves don't last forever; they constantly rise to fall - this too shall pass.

When I experienced the loss of my child, I learned the importance of surrender. My friend, once again I've suffered to know what it feels like to suffer - to gain compassion. This was all for you. That wave in my life allowed me to see the big picture. My life doesn't belong to me. It's a shell tossed to and fro by the hands of God. There's no need to be bitter about the things you cannot change. It only makes matters worse. All we can do is surrender and let the waves carry us to the place of rest and plenty.

It's not an accident. It's no coincidence. You're to gain from this experience. It's your responsibility to find out what. Help others gain from this experience. The wave is equipping you to become. It's building your character. It's setting right some wrongs. It's moving you closer to a new beginning.

Trust *The* Great Spirit. He knows what He's doing. Every challenge, every setback, every disappointment - heartache; are waves being stilled by the hands of God. My friend, you're about to witness divine intervention in your life. You've surrendered. You finally let go to let God. You're about to wash up onto your new beginning. No worries. It may seem scary at first; nonetheless, once you explore the land you'll see its potential. You'll see plenty of room to build. This territory is abundant. It's larger than the ditch you were stuck in before.

Let the old you stay at sea. Embrace the new you. Be confident. Know who you are. You are a precious jewel: worth far more than rubies, the fowls in the air, the fish in the sea, and the rodents that creep and crawl upon the earth. Therefore, *The* Great Spirit will settle for nothing less than the best beneficial outcome for you.

Surrender. Let the waves in your life carry you where you need to be. Flow to prevent further friction. This is how you surf the waves. Do this my love: and you'll wash up on dry, fertile, abundant land; flowing with milk and honey: to nourish the spirit.

You're Treasure To Be Found

Chapter Ten:
Climb Out

We've all made mistakes in our lives. We'll continue to do so. We're not perfect. We all have regrets, emotional breaks, face temptation, suffer the consequences of bad decisions; and will grow tired at some point or another. We all face challenges, all have doubts, and struggle to overcome obstacles. My friends, In spite of it all: know you are loved.

Too many people go through life thinking nobody loves them. Feeling left out, unnoticed, ignored, abandoned, rejected, unwanted, and alone. They find themselves victims of cruelty and unfair treatment. My friend, you're never alone. You'll always be loved. God loves you, I love you, and no matter what flaws you may or may not have: you should love yourself.

Don't get use to those feelings. Don't let your emotions tell you who you are. Don't identify yourself as their victim. No. Don't let issues of the flesh define who you are. The flesh is not who you are; it's what you wear. It's a well-constructed piece of clothing - It can be damaged. The flesh gets dirty and requires cleansing; it gets cut and needs stitching; it can be burned into ashes and cease to exist: this is not so with spirit. My friend, know who you are: you are spirit. Yes. You are love. You are beautiful just the way you are. Love yourself.

Doesn't matter how you dress your situation up: it's still there. It doesn't matter how you wear the mask: it's still a mask. You can put on all the makeup you want and they'll still call you ugly - this you are not. You're beautiful inside and out. Love yourself. Nobody on earth can do this better than you.

Believe in you. Trust you. Accept you. Get to know you. My friend, until you do this, your status in life will remain. You'll continue to let others walk all over you. Why? Because you do not love you. You'll continue to settle. Why? Because you do not love you. You'll continue to embrace negativity. Why? Because you do not love you. You'll continue to think you're not worthy. Why? Because you do not love you.

I DON'T CARE... what *they* say or have said about you. Light of the world, I'm telling you: it's a lie. Don't believe *their* lies. When you don't love you; you give others control over you. You let them use your insecurities against you. My friend, when you love yourself; you'll see *them* for who, or, what they truly are - distraction. You'll never be good enough for this person. They'll continue to try to drag you down: don't let them.

God never said you had to look a certain way for Him to use you. He never said you had to walk or talk a certain way for Him to love you. No. He loves you unconditionally the way you are. Maybe you're not educated. Maybe you've made some bad choices. Maybe you carry around extra weight. You're loved. Maybe you were born with deformity. Maybe you walk with a limp. Maybe you're religious; or, you believe nothing at all. You're loved. Maybe you're light skinned. Maybe you're dark skinned. Guess what? None of that matters. You're still loved. You still deserve to be loved and respected. Yes. You're worthy of love.

You have a valid reason for feeling the way you do. The world is a cold dark place even when the sun is shining. Some people are just mean and hateful. They say stuff to hurt you. Be of good cheer my love. What they say is not about you, their unhappy with themselves. They'll mock you in public to gain praise. They feel the need to be validated. No. This is not about you. It's about their own fear and insecurity with themselves. They struggle with ego. Believe it or not, they want what you have.

You don't need to seek validation from others; you're validated by God. Words, laughter, and finger pointing will not stop what *The* Great Spirit's started; it'll only kindle His wrath. When God created you, He began creating a masterpiece. He's not finished with you yet. There's still work to be done. Like any artist, God loves His work of art.

There'll always be people trying to make you feel bad about yourself. There'll always be people trying to stop your progress through intimidation. There'll always be people who'd rather choose harsh words over kind gestures. There'll always be people who think they're in control and know better than God. These people are of this world. My friend, you're not of this world. You carry *Greatness* inside you.

If you're to become the masterpiece God's created you to become; you can't worry about what other people think. You can't get stuck in believing everything people say to you about you. You have to love yourself enough to want what's best for you.I may not always agree with what you do; nonetheless, that'll never stop me from loving you. When we as a whole begin to understand love is what matters: we'll take back what belongs to us.

My friend, when you feel unloved; question the feeling. Ask yourself where the feeling is coming from. What issues have you allowed to sit inside you too long? What's stopping you from loving you? Why are you full of self-doubt? Why are you full of self-hate? Why do you curse your existence? Why do you neglect yourself? Why do you overeat? Why do you cut yourself? You're unhappy with you. Why? Because you do not love yourself. Why? Because you don't know who you are.

Stop it. Stop making things worse. Stop delaying your growth. Get to know yourself. Fall in love with you. You're the only thing standing between you and the best God has for you. You already have His love. He's waiting for you to begin to love yourself. He knows what you look like. He knows the mistakes you've made. He knows the level of your talents. He knows what happened. He knows your issues. He knows your struggles. He's turning things around! Do your part. Get out of your head. Quiet the noise around you. Start loving yourself like God loves you.

Don't be so harsh and unforgiving towards yourself. Don't go through life putting yourself through unnecessary suffering. Love yourself. God will finish the masterpiece He started in you.

All the people who laugh at you and call you names; all the people who betrayed and abandoned you; all the people who pushed you down and placed a heel on your head: will be repaid by God. Yes. All the people who kicked you while you were down and spat on you; all the people who told you you'll never be nothing: all of them have caused you pain, and all of them will get what's due. Be of good cheer my friend.

Get up. Stand tall. Hold your head up high. Keep stepping! Keep moving towards the *Goal*. Don't let it stop you. Quit believing what *they* say. Move forward. Look in the mirror to see the truth. You're not ugly: you're a masterpiece in the making. You're not worthless. No. You're greatly valued.

I have a message of hope for you today my love: God loves you and so do I. Love yourself.

Maybe you're feeling unlovable. My friend, change the way you think. Get rid of that thought before it takes root. Thinking like that will cause you to push anyone who tries to get close to you away. It'll cause you to act out in ways not beneficial for your good.

There was a time I felt I wasn't loved because I wasn't lovable. It was around the time I tried to kill myself. I felt ugly, hopeless, miserable, and alone. Yes. I felt I was a mistake and deeply flawed. *Why can't I just be normal?* I'd ask. *Why can't I just get it right? Why? Why? Why? Why me?* My friends, I climbed into a ditch so full of self-pity; it took a divine hand to pull me out. I'm grateful. I was about to drown in a lie.

I wasn't seeing things clearly. I was so deep in that lie: I couldn't see God had His hands on me. I know what He said; however, I could no longer see evidence of Him working in my life. Yes. I believed He turned me over to a reprobate mind.

I began to hate everything about me. I'd completely forgotten who I was. There were days I didn't know my own name. I had to begin again. I had to get lost to be found. I had to be hated to know what it feels like to be loved. I didn't know; but now, I know I'm loved by God in spite of it all. The world's love doesn't compare - it disappoints. The world's love will tell you: "I love you *but you need to* look a certain way. You need to have *this or that*. I'm not in love with you. I think we should see other people." My friends, the world's love is not unconditional; it's greedy for gain: it has requirements. *The* Great Spirit loves us unconditionally in spite of all our faults.

No amount of money is going to make you happy. Finding a partner and acquiring friends is not going to make you happy. Complaining is not going to make you happy. No. Smothering yourself with temporary success will not make you happy. In fact, it may make things worse.

Climb Out

That wound is infected. You're going to need to clean it out before it gets better. Get rid limiting beliefs you have about yourself. Yes. My friend, get rid of self-inflicting habits. Quiet the noise. Spend some time getting to know you; the real you, the only true and lasting you. You are love. That in which you seek is closer than you think. Make the choice to love you. Stop making up excuses as to why you don't deserve to be loved. If you didn't deserve to be loved; God would not have placed it inside of you. Climb out of the ditch of self-pity before you drown. Love yourself.

You want someone to notice you. You want attention. You feel trapped in yourself. Take the time to notice you. Give yourself attention. Set yourself free. Maybe you need help. You want help; but instead of going to find help, you expect help to find you. No. Stop sitting down in that ditch of self-pity. Climb out and go get the help you need. My friend, you have divine help: ask for it.

You may be tempted to think: "If I looked a certain way things would be better. If only I had a different life I would be better off. If I had her beauty and his charm people would love me." My friend, all outward beauty fades in time; it's the beauty from within that never greys or wrinkles. This is the beauty to seek and find. This is love in the purest form: undiluted by the hands of man.

Once you decide to be who you are: love; you'll be able to recognize it in others. If you think your life doesn't matter; I am telling you now: you're wrong. You're stuck in a ditch of self-pity. Climb Out! Here is your ladder: God loves you and so do I.

Who wants to fall in and out of love? I don't. That's exhausting - just love. The unconditional love God has for us; is the same unconditional love we should have for ourselves and each other.

My friend, you can't see His vision for you as the masterpiece: it's beautiful. It may seem like others are a completed work of art; but they're not finished yet either. Don't compare yourself to what they got going on. Don't compare the *Vase with Fifteen Flowers* to the *Mona Lisa*. They are two totally different paintings. Yes, both are beautiful; but one is bright flowers in a vase. You can always go outside and see a flower; but something so rare and unique: where can you find it again? Which do you think in time is valued more?

In spite of it all, God loves you. In spite of it all, love yourself. My friend, climb out of the pit of self-pity. Start living the life you want. If no one has ever taken time to be a friend to you; take the time to be a friend to someone else. If no one has invited you to their barbeque; have your own barbeque. Invite the poor to celebrate with you; you'll form friendships that are lasting.

You see my friend, the poor do not judge. They're grateful someone took the time to care about them. They don't care about what you look like. They don't care how you talk. They don't care what you did back then. They don't care that you're, "not educated enough." They see you for who you are: love. So if you want love, my friend, be love. This shouldn't be hard; because you are love. You are what you seek. Stop hiding yourself.

I hear you: "I have no family. I have no friends. I feel empty. I'm tired. I want to end this pain and misery now." Stop it. Climb out of self-pity and go get the life you want. There are opportunities lined up for you: you can't see because you're stuck in a ditch.

Hope To A Friend Sunrise

My friend, make the choice to love you no matter where you are in life. If you don't have the strength, lean on God. You may be weak; but, He's always strong. He will lift, hold you up, and carry you the rest of the way. What's man's support; when you have God's support?

Climb out of that ditch. Yes. Dust yourself off. You've been in there too long. You're malnourished. The negative voices in your head are out powering the positive voices. It shouldn't be this way. Quiet the noise. Those negative voices in your head are making matters worse. They're causing your circumstances to look bigger; or worse than they really are. Once you stop listening to all the chatter going on in your mind; and begin to follow your heart: pain and the feeling of inadequacy will dissolve. You are enough.

All people aren't created evil. There's still some good in the world - we just have to squint our eyes to see it. My friends, light shines on top of the mountain where love will be found abundant. You don't have to lock yourself away. It wasn't meant for you to be hidden. Let your light shine for all men to see. You're beautifully and wonderfully made. You're a masterpiece in progress. Yes. You're a masterpiece in the making. Love yourself.

Change what you tell you about you. Instead of telling yourself: "I'm a failure. I'm fat. I'm dumb. I'm ugly. I'm weird. I'll never make it." Start telling yourself: "I have what it takes. I'm deserving. I'm competent. I'm enough. I'm worthy. I'm valuable. I'm lovable. I am loved. I am love. I love myself!"

Stop treating yourself badly. Be fair to yourself. You don't have to live a lonely life locked away from others. You don't have to punish yourself for something you didn't do wrong in the first place. You don't have to settle for what you think you deserve, based on what others say. Climb out of that ditch. Go get the life you want. You're not an object to be used; you're a masterpiece in the making.

You're too valuable to go through life not knowing your own worth. You're too valuable to go through life believing you're nothing. My friend, you're not invisible. God sees you. There's hope for your future. Don't give up on your dreams. Don't get distracted from your purpose. Dust yourself off. Arise!

You feel incomplete. You feel you don't fit in. You feel like you're standing naked in the cold: embarrassed, humiliated, devastated, ashamed, and depressed. Maybe you were violated, discouraged, and placed in a box. You feel limited and stuck. Climb out! Take charge of your life. Start making necessary changes.

My friend, *The* Great Spirit's picking up the pieces. Yes. He's putting the old, broken, seemingly useless you back together again. Glory! He's making you whole again. Yes. He's increasing your value. Stop people pleasing. Stop relying on people to complete the masterpiece God started. They don't have His vision for you. They don't have His precision. They'll just leave you hanging high and dry. God will position you in favor; that others may marvel at His good work. You don't need them. My friend, get out of your head; and when you go, take everybody else with you.

Material things will not make you feel better about yourself. Alcohol's not going to make you feel better about yourself. Drugs won't make you feel better about yourself. Sex isn't going to make you feel better about yourself. Stop trying to be perfect. It's okay to be a work in progress. Stop trying to prove yourself to others. You've already been approved. My friend, you're not going to find the solution to your problem in that ditch. There's no need for you to mope around with a bad attitude; in a bad mood, feeling sorry for yourself. Doing this won't solve the problem. Take action.

Climb out of self-pity. Yes. Dust off anything holding you back from loving you: limiting beliefs about yourself, fear of failure, feelings of inadequacy, low self-esteem, self-loathing behaviors, and negative experiences. Maybe you've made a mistake. It's okay. We all do. Don't be so hard on yourself. Don't try to float through life on pieces of a raft: you have a boat.

My friend, *The* Great Spirit's taking the time to fill in your void. He's mapping out corners to enlarge your territory. He's adding shape and color to your life. He's completing the masterpiece He started when He made you. Trust Him. You're going to turn out the way you should. Beautiful work of art!

We all get down in the ditch of self-pity at some point or another; however, we're not supposed to stay down there. Climb to see the opportunities lined up for you. God knows what He's doing. Yes. He knew there'd be lines crossed before He started painting the picture.

Hope To A Friend Sunrise

Things are going to be okay my friend - if you let them be okay. Make the choice to love you no matter what.

Be bold. Tell yourself: "I'm not going to drown in the ditch of self-pity. I will not let negative people keep me down. I will not keep myself down by holding onto emotional weight. I'm going to climb out. I'm going to go get the life I want. I'm going to walk through the line of opportunities God's drawn out for me. I'm going to love myself in spite of what I look like, if no one else does, in spite of my character, in spite of mistakes I've made, in spite of insecurities: I'm climbing out!"

You believe you're alone. My friend, put your shoulders back and hold your head up high. You're covered in the lies of self-pity. You're not alone. There are others in the ditch with you. Use each other to climb out. You were not destined to die in that ditch.

You think the task is too hard. You think the ditch is too deep. You can't see how things will ever get better for you. You can't see love. My friend, there's hope for your future. If you've found a way into the ditch: you know the way out. Change the way you view things. Start climbing higher. Grab hold of something solid. Dig your way out. Love is there. Love is always going to be right where you are. Why? Because you are love.

You are not unwanted. There's someone looking for you. This person hasn't found you because you're not in a good place to be found. You're hiding in a ditch. Climb out!

You've been told time after time in some form or another: "You're not good enough. You're destined to fail. I don't love you." No. Don't let those words weigh you down in the ditch. They're just words. Although words hurt; and for a time can keep you captive: the truth will set you free. What is the truth? God loves you and so do I. You are love. Love yourself. Climb out! When you love you; you teach others how to love you. Set the standard.

You feel useless. You hate living. You feel like ending it. You feel like no one cares about you. Negativity's raining down on you my friend. That ditch is flooded with lies. You're not useless. You're a masterpiece in the making. You're greatly valued. Your life matters. Start swimming to the top my love.

Someone has taught you to feel the way you do. Someone has taught you how to get stuck. No disrespect; but you're being taught by a bad teacher. Go find a good teacher and learn how to get unstuck.

When I'm called names, I think about Whoopi in *The Color Purple*. After hearing everything negative from *Mister*, Her last response to him was: "Everything you done to me, already done to you, I'm poor, black, I may even be ugly; but dear God I'm here. I'm here." My friend, this should be your new attitude.

You are here. Live in that truth. It doesn't matter if you're black, white, purple, orange, or blue: you're here. It doesn't matter if you're fat or skinny: you're here. It doesn't matter if you're tall or short: you're here. It doesn't matter if you talk straight or stutter: you're here. It doesn't matter if you're rich or poor: you're here. You've made some mistakes; my friend, it doesn't matter: you're still here. God didn't name any creation ugly. From my view, it's all beautiful; they're all beautiful; you're all beautiful: a masterpiece in the making. Don't pay them any mind. Know who you are for you. You are love, you're loved, and you are loveable. Love yourself.

My friend, do for others; but, don't expect others to do for you. If they do that's fine. I'm not telling you to walk away from help when help is needed. I'm not telling you to turn down gifts. No. Don't go into anything wanting something in return. Don't do something for someone out of the goodness of your heart; then expect them to pay the price for something they didn't ask for: or couldn't afford in the first place. This is how you let yourself down. This is how you start feeling no one cares.

You've spent your life helping others; however, when you needed help: the people you've helped didn't help you. People only seem to call you when they want or need something. You'll find yourself saying, *"I do this, I do that, I did this, I did that, but no one has ever done the same for me."* My friend, watch your step! Next thing you know you'll be saying, *"no one cares."* Then, you wake up one morning in a ditch of self-pity. If you're going to do it, then do it; but do it for you and leave it at that. Some people are selfish. Don't let that keep you down in the ditch. Be you in spite of - love. Your heart is what makes you special. It's what separates the *Vase with Fifteen Flowers* from the *Mona Lisa*. You have a calling placed on your life. People are attracted to your spirit. Use this to your advantage.

You don't have to want for anything: *The* Great Spirit's taken care of it; but you're brothers and sisters are in need of sustenance – feed them.

My friend, climb out of that ditch. No matter what comes your way: don't let it push you back down. Don't get offended. Remember my love; what they're saying isn't about you. No. Don't get bitter, angry, ashamed, or down on yourself. Don't walk around with a chip on your shoulder. What they do to you is already done to them. Be of good cheer. *The* Great Spirit's painting over some negative issues in your life: to give you a better view. I wish you could see what I see – it is beautiful.

You think you're a dreadful person. You think no one could possibly love you. You don't even know what it means to love in order to recognize it. You've lost all confidence in yourself. Maybe you blame others for the bad choices you've made. You're saying, "If I had better parents this wouldn't have happened." Don't put that burden on them. What happened to you was out of their control. They were not there - you were. You made the choice to do what you did. Accept it, get up, and move on. It's in the past: climb out and leave it there.

Climb Out

You're faced with a choice: either climb out of self-pity to go live the life you want; or stay stuck in destructive negative emotions with resentment, feeling bitter and sorry for yourself. My friend, It'll get crowded in that ditch. Why would you want to stay down there? There's nothing there for you. There's no food to give you energy, no drink to fill your thirst, no blankets to keep you warm: no covering to protect you from the storm raining lies.

It's okay to be down for a little while, just make sure you know where the stairs are to get back up. However, as long as you're in that ditch; your thoughts are in control. You'll find yourself worrying about things that don't even matter. You'll find yourself willing to stop trying; willing to stop living; willing to give up on hope. You'll allow others to walk all over you. You'll become timid and reserved within: afraid to speak because thoughts overpower. My friend, quiet the noise. Climb out of self-pity. Take back your life!

Allow yourself to live. You are not living in that ditch – you're stuck. You were not created to be defeated. Get up! Get out! Go! Start Climbing! There's more out there for you. I know it's not easy. Whoever told you it would be lied to your face. No. It's not easy: it's necessary. It's necessary for growth. It's necessary for forward movement. Get out of that bed. Get out of that house. You are beautiful. My friend, you don't have to hide. Let go of the weight holding you down. Yes my love, swim to the top. Breathe!

You're caught on a lie and the knife to cut yourself free is in your hands. You have what it takes. You're enough. Stop holding yourself hostage: refusing to let you free - refusing to let you live. Time is not stopping. Your life is going to fly by while you're in that ditch. If you're lucky enough to be seen; it will wave at you from the distance. My friend, don't waste another minute of your life down in the dumps. Rise above it all.

Stop making excuses as to why you don't deserve to have the life you want. Stop making excuses as to why you don't deserve to be loved; why you don't deserve to be happy; why you don't deserve to be respected. Why don't you deserve to succeed? No. Don't drown in the lies. We're all faced with challenges. We've all been disappointed at some point or another. Don't let it keep you down. Don't let self-pity keep you from your destiny. My friend, do your part: cut yourself lose from negativity. Start the climb. Don't believe everything everyone tells you about you. Know who you are. You are a masterpiece in the making. You're beautiful the way you are. Go get the life you want. If you want love: be love.

My dear friend, you are love, you are loved, and you are lovable. Start being you. Start loving yourself. Put this book down. Go find a mirror. When you find that mirror, I want you to take a good look at yourself and say: *I love you.* Don't worry about who may be watching you. Take this time for yourself. Let *you* know in spite of everything you've been told; in spite of your history, in spite of your flaws: *you* love *you.* Be who you are my love. Walk with your head held high. Know the truth of your existence You are love.

My friend, where are you? If you find yourself stuck in the ditch of self-pity; climb out. Be of good cheer my love. Be free. Yes. Start living. If you need help, here's your ladder: God loves you and so do I.

You Are Love

Hope deferred makes the heart sick,

but a longing fulfilled is a tree of life

Proverbs 13:12 (NIV)

Chapter Eleven:
Penny for Dollars

I recall thinking a penny was worth more than a dollar. Why wouldn't it be? It shined. I didn't see the value in something I could scribble all over: something that was easy to get wet; something easy for me to tear to pieces. Pennies are made of metal. They'll last longer than a printed piece of cotton fibered paper. Although at a young age I learned to value the penny; with time, I had to sacrifice some pennies for dollars.

Dollars are worth more. People go to great lengths for dollars. Some people will even lie, cheat, and steal for grand collection of them. Yes. They value the dollar more than life itself. But money is not my focus. My focus is sacrifice.

Sacrifice is a requirement for growth. Throughout the different stages of life; you're going to have to let somethings go. The apostle Paul touched base on such a requirement when he said: "When I was a child, I spake as a child, I understood as a child, I thought as a child: but when I became a man, I put away childish things." He was magnifying his sacrifice.

No. I'm not talking about the slaughter of an animal. Blood shed has a voice - it cries out from the ground for justice. No. Be merciful and love. Your burnt offerings are no longer enough. You don't have to sacrifice the lamb. It's done. My friend, there's still sacrifice to make: whether it's time, energy, possession, relationship, emotion, convenience, comfort, or ego.

If something's easy to sacrifice it's not sacrifice. Your sacrifice should make you uncomfortable at the very thought of it. It comes from within - not without. My friend, you are your sacrifice. I eco the words spoken before: "Present your bodies a living sacrifice, holy, acceptable unto God, which is your reasonable service." You may prefer to walk around the edges to avoid the middle; but doing so, you'll never be able to get to the center of it all. You must make the necessary moves towards your destiny.

Trade in some of your pennies. *The* Great Spirit promises to give you dollars in return - dollars He'll multiply greatly. What you're trying to collect for yourself, has less value than what *The* Great Spirit's stored up for you.

My friend, let go of the weight: you're swimming in deep waters. Sacrifice to get to the best God has for you. I know this is the hardest part for you. It's not supposed to be easy. I know it's frustrating - heartbreaking. Wait my friend. Before you start crying over spoiled milk; realize, now you can make cheese. Not just cheese: you can make something sweet out of something sour, bad smelling, and bitter tasting to your spirit. What many people pour down the drain doesn't have to be wasted in your life.

You don't have to get rid of all your pennies. Some pennies are worth more than dollars - in rare cases. Besides, too much sacrifice without the presence of reward leads to resentment.

My friend, to make a dollar a hundred pennies are needed in exchange. You can cash in your pennies for something more valuable. In the same way, every sacrifice you make is your way of cashing in on your dreams. You can't see it now; but your sacrifice will be worth it in the end.

"Moses, when he was come to years, refused to be called the son of Pharaoh's daughter; choosing rather to suffer affliction with the people of God, than to enjoy the pleasures of sin for a season." In other words, Moses sacrificed pennies for dollars. Sure, things may have looked promising at the time. Those mountains of coins looked like an arrival at true success; but Moses could see past the surface of the matter. Yes. He knew something had to be done - so he did it. He sacrificed and cashed in.

The Great Spirit is the banker with all the funding you need. He pays interest. He's going to be fair in His dealings with you. You might have to make some uncomfortable decisions. You may have to walk away. You might have to quit your job and move. My friend, you may have to sacrifice getting your way this time. No worries. Be of good cheer. Your next statement from God will be sufficient. What *The* Great Spirit's stored up for you is more than you could ever store up for yourself.

I've learned you can't get everything you want in life; but, you can get everything you need. It's tough to give up certain things. My friend, look at the bigger picture. The level of happiness you'll achieve when you make appropriate sacrifice; weighs on the scale of success, and outweighs the sense of failure.

Yes my friend, you may have to leave some friends and family behind. Be of good cheer. No worries. All will be well. Reaching your destination in life depends on how badly you want to. It's hard to adjust to the changes at first. However, you'll enjoy your new situation once you adjust. My dear friend, when you're happy: your life is happy. Your family will get better. You'll meet new people. You'll experience new things. Yes. Be of good cheer my love. Don't be dismayed. You'll make new memories. Make the sacrifice. Your decision not to sacrifice could cause you to sink into depression and regret. Take the time to better *you* - for *you*.

My friend, sacrificing takes courage. You'll need to be willing to go the extra mile. You might even have to start at the bottom. No worries. You can work your way up. I've never known a journey that didn't start behind where one begins.

I'd say when you sacrifice nothing you get nothing; but, it isn't true. You'll get something. However, it'll be less than you're worth. If you don't walk away from that abusive relationship; you'll continue to get those black eyes. I didn't say walk out of your marriage. I wouldn't tell you to do that. I only suggest you stand your ground. Yes. Take root in your purpose to become in spite of. Let the spirit move you. You might need to spend time alone. Don't worry about what he or she's doing: focus on you. Let what will *be - be*.

My dear friend, your sacrifice is not your punishment. You don't have to sacrifice your health, family, or integrity. That type of sacrifice isn't meant for everybody. No. Don't use this to escape responsibility. You have a responsibility to your husband. You have a responsibility to your children. You have a responsibility to your wife. You're responsible for your child. My friend in your case, if it doesn't feel right: it's not right.

You're them and they're you. If you walk out on them; you're walking out on you. Your wife is your blessing: she's not a penny. She's not even a dollar. Yes. She's worth more than even that. Your husband is your blessing: he's not a penny. He's not even a dollar. Yes. He's worth more than that. My friend, if you must sacrifice something in regards to responsibility: let it be your pride and ego. Nothing pleases *The* Great Spirit more than love. If you cannot love the flesh of your flesh; where does your love begin? Focus on what matters - love.

The Pennies in your life are things holding you back from the best God has for you. They're bad associations, impurities in character, outdated attitudes, negative emotions, and daily irritations. These are the areas where sacrifice is needed. They may not start off like this; but, over time pennies do oxidize and become old and rusty looking. You can save them in your penny bank; however, you don't have to carry them around with you.

Although sacrifice is a requirement for both change and growth: it's a choice. You can choose to remain where you are. You can choose to trade in your dollars for pennies. My friends, beware: too many pennies will weigh you down.

Sacrifice. God's waiting for you to make the next move. The deposit's been made. He's waiting for you to make the withdrawal. Every time we're faced with opposition, we need to remind ourselves: "These are only pennies. There's more stored up for me. *The* Great Spirit's deposited a greater blessing in my name."

You might have to sacrifice sleep, time, money, old ways of thinking, and bad ways of acting. My friend, "What doesn't kill you will make you stronger." The type of sacrifice I'm encouraging you to make is not meant to kill you. It's meant to help you develop. It's meant to help you reach the next level of being. Yes. It's meant to make you stronger.

Sacrifice is the weight to achieving strength in the life we want. It's our way of building on the desire for more. It's our way of making the decision not to delay, defer, or give up. It's our way of making the withdrawal. Sacrifice some people's predictions and assumptions. You shouldn't be afraid to live your life because of what someone else has told you in your past; you'll become in your future. It's your life. They have their own life to live. How can they focus on them and you and be accurate? Yes my friend, sacrifice your habit of trying to please everybody: it's wearing you down.

It's possible to sacrifice and not get what's desired in return. Pray all you want; however, you can't get everything you want: "What looks good aint always good for you." *The* Great Spirit refuses to let you settle for anything less than the best He has for you. You asked why: that's why. You're in the wrong profession - try again.

You may say: "My husband gets on my nerves. He's inconsiderate. He's grouchy. I don't have to put up with this. I want a divorce." Have you ever viewed your situation to be a test of your faith? Do not be moved. Suffer it to be so now. Things are going to turn to work out in your favor. Be patient. My friend, be of service. Let this be your sacrifice.

What you sacrifice to reach your goal is up to you. It's your personal choice. You'll deal with the consequences of the decisions you make. Therefore my love, think before you act; and act before you think too long.

There are variables to consider. Always question the importance of your sacrifice. Forecast the difficulty of the challenge. Forecast your victory. Where are you going to start? When are you going to start? What's your current situation? How much time do you need to achieve your desired outcome? Do you have a support system? Do you have the resources? This way, you're at least somewhat prepared for what will come - temptation.

My friend, it's difficult to let go. However, if you let go; what does that say about you? You're stronger than you think. You're worth more than you know. Yes. You're worth more than stuff. Don't allow obsession to hold you captive. Don't let addiction pin you down. Break free! Fly home my friend. Flap your wings in faith and fly home.

If you don't make the appropriate sacrifices when necessary; you're at risk of sacrificing yourself. If you're not willing to give up some pennies for dollars: there's a good chance you'll be weighed down by the stressors of this world. My friend, shed the weight. Move towards the goal. If you aren't willing to give something up to reach your goal; there's the possibility you'll never get there.

I sacrifice daily, because I'm tempted daily. I'm tempted to settle. I'm tempted to give up. I'm tempted to think bad about myself. Yes. I'm tempted to curse some people out. But you know what? I say to myself: *If I fail, I'll at least fail trying not to fail* - in that way I succeed. My friend, if you study your ways without cease; you'll become proficient in you. Once you become proficient in you, the problem regarding you is easier to solve. Hence the words spoken before: "Know thyself."

Sacrifice and surrender are not the same. To sacrifice is to do your part. To surrender is to let God do His part. My friend, if you don't do the work; how do you expect to get paid? If you don't take the time to make a withdrawal; how do you expect to receive? Make the effort to get your desired outcome.

Sacrifice isn't Gods way of trying to break you. He's not trying to take everything from you. No. He's not. He's trying to give you more. *The* Great Spirit knows a deposit of His favor was made in your name. He's waiting for you to make the withdrawal.

The only way we can withdraw from the ATM of grace, is through sacrifice. Let go of the attitudes weighing you down. Put the knife to the throat of your ego. Get rid of stuff that no longer serves your purpose. No. Don't identifying with stuff. Yes. Be willing to sacrifice harsh words. Set yourselves apart from the world; if only but for a moment: to hear from Him. Sacrifice some pennies for dollars.

Have a little talk with self. Tell self: "I'm willing to do what it takes. I'm willing to compromise my way. I'm willing to train. I'm willing to take the time. I'm willing to study. I'm willing to reach my goal. Yes. I'm able to reach my goal. I won't allow pennies to way me down. I'm going to make the appropriate sacrifice. I know God's made a deposit in my name. I'm going to withdraw from the ATM of His grace."

My friend, sacrifice that guilt. I dare you to stop focusing on regret and shame. Start looking with eyes of hope towards your future. Stop letting the issues of your past manipulate and control your mind - and therefore your actions. The guilt you're carrying with you is worthless. It's not even a penny. It has no worth. It adds no value to your life. It will cost you more when it's all said and done. Make room in your life for things of value.

I challenge you to sacrifice your fear; this too is worthless weight. It'll hold you back from getting what belongs to you. Instead of playing it safe, venture out. Meet the opportunity.

I challenge you to sacrifice anger and resentment. Let go of those unwanted pounds of hurt. It's not good for your health. It's dead weight. My friend, it's not needed. Instead of keeping you warm, it'll make you cold and bitter. Release it! Move on to your future.

To become, you have to let go of the thing with the lesser value: to obtain true value. You'll have to lose to gain. You may have to suffer through some uncomfortable situations. You might have to go without. My dear friend, suffer it to be so now. There's a deposit in your name.

Do your part. Let go of what you're not supposed to hold onto. Be willing to take a walk in faith. Yes. Exercise away dead weight. You'll get in return something desired more than wealth, fame, or pleasure. This is a promise. It has been written: "Eye hath not seen, nor ear heard, neither have entered into the heart of man, the things which God hath prepared for them that love Him."

You might not understand why; but you'll discover every obstacle you've overcome: *worthwhile*. Yes. To overcome you have to sacrifice. Get rid of some pennies, so *The* Great Spirit can bless you with dollars.

Stop holding onto what you can't take with you; grasp, as an infant, the beneficial things you can. My friend, no matter what the flesh speaks to your spirit: this world is not your home. You've taken ownership of another man's house; when He returns, you better not be found sleeping. Arise! Take your place!

Sacrifice. Demand your inheritance. Sacrifice what's difficult and the difficulty will cease. Sacrifice the sorrow and hope you'll see. Yes. Sacrifice the affliction of addiction, and your soul will rest in peace.

The Great Spirit's fulfilling every promise He made to you. He's heard every word you've mumbled. Every whisper sounded as a trumpet in His ear. Don't waste time, energy, or concern on the things that don't matter. When life gets tough; when you feel weighed down by the stressors of this world; when you're overwhelmed by stuff: remember, these are pennies you can trade for dollars.

When so called friends turn their backs on you; remember: these are pennies. When you get fired from the job you've worked at for over ten years without notice; remember: these are pennies. When your husband or wife takes everything and leaves you with seemingly nothing; remember: it's a pocket of pennies. Be of good cheer my love. God has more stored up for you. Your story is not supposed to end on a sad note. As I've often heard my mama say: "Tell it like it T I is." My friend, tell it victoriously.

You've learned what you needed to learn from that situation. Now, it's time to pass the test and move on to the next level. Don't fight against your blessings. Make the appropriate sacrifice. Yes. Withdraw from the ATM of God's grace. Sacrifice that hurt. Sacrifice disbelief. My friend, stay in faith. Walk in integrity with your head up high. Your greater has been deposited. Go get it!

I don't know everything God's deposited in your life; but it's all good. It's all to help you grow. Look inside yourself. Search the various regions of your heart. My friend, find what you need. Gather what you need from the heart. The sooner you make the appropriate sacrifice, the better off you'll be. Dump out some pennies. Yes. Cash in some pennies for dollars. You may have your favorites; you may have too many to choose from; remember: the more you keep the more you carry.

As long as you're carrying the weight of your problems; you're taking ownership of something that doesn't belong to you. Your worries are not *yours* to worry about. My friend, "Cast thy burden upon God, and He shall sustain thee: He shall never suffer the righteous to be moved." Light of the world, you shall not be moved by the hands of man. *The* Great Spirit will move you to fertile ground.

We pray for God to show up; however, we can't even seem to arrive on time. By the time we get there, *The* Great Spirit's performed the miracle and moved on. Why are you late? I'll tell you why. You're too busy trying to count pennies. By the time you get to the door of opportunity it's closed. No worries. No need to be down on yourself. When one door of opportunity closes, another door of opportunity opens. No. Don't allow yourself to be distracted by pennies. Arrive on time.

Make the appropriate sacrifice. Every time you sacrifice and overcome; you become stronger than before. You realize you can live without. You realize: lust and greed didn't have as much power over you as you thought. You realize it's easy to say no. You realize it's easy to walk away. You realize you're able to make hard decisions. Yes. You realize you have what it takes to pass your test. You've sacrificed your selfishness. You've grabbed hold to selflessness. You chose not to settle for a lie. You chose to do your part. You chose to make the withdrawal. Now, you're rich in spirit.

Your statement with God reads: "Better than before, stronger, wiser, healed, delivered, righteous and redeemed: favored with a total sum of blessed." Yes. The way your story's supposed to end. And these are but a few things *The* Great Spirit has deposited in your life: there's more.

You'll feel relieved when you empty out your pockets. Don't carry around anything that doesn't serve your purpose. If distraction or hoard is found; make the appropriate sacrifice. When things get heavy in life;

when weighed down by the issues of the world: cash in some pennies for dollars.

My friend, *The* Great Spirit has a blessing with your name on it. He's made a deposit of favor in the ATM of grace for you. Will you make the withdrawal today?

Do What It Takes; Make The Sacrifice.

Chapter Twelve:
Stay in Line

I was in line waiting to eat breakfast at a restaurant. I was hungry. It felt like my stomach was trying to crawl out of my body. People were standing around outside. Every time the door swung open; one group of customers would leave out and another group would walk in. It was a slow process. My friend and I were last in line. We waited over a half hour before becoming anxious.

I tried to be patient. I couldn't convince my stomach to do the same. There was another restaurant down the street. We decided to go there instead. We were convinced they wouldn't have a line. We were wrong. Consequently, we ended up having to wait longer than before. Standing in line I heard a voice scream to my spirit, ""Wait your turn." Light of the world, now I speak loudly to your spirit: stay in line, be patient, and wait your turn.

Before *The* Great Spirit gave you breath of life, He set things according to your life in perfect order. He lined up your experiences, relationships, circumstances: every door on your path. He purposely positioned the right people, the right breaks, and the right opportunities: to all happen at the right time. *The* Great Spirit has your arrival planned out. Yes. Your arrival to happiness. Your arrival to good health. Your arrival to marriage. Your arrival to acceptance. Your arrival to success. It's in the stream.

On the way to your destiny, there'll be times you'll have to find shelter from the rain. Wait for the storm to cease. There'll be times you'll have to stop to allow another to pass. My friend, there'll be times when you'll have to stand in long lines for hours; just to be told to wait a little longer. Be of good cheer. It's about to be your turn.

People get frustrated and discouraged by what they can't see: causing them to get out of line prematurely.

They give up on hope. They quit trying. They assume: "It will never happen for me." My friend, don't expect things to happen when you want them to. Expect things to work out for your good. I know the waiting game seems like forever. Things are difficult right now. Stay in line. It's about to be your turn.

You've studied hard and taken the test multiple times; nonetheless, you can't seem to get a passing grade. You keep putting in the applications for employment; however, no one is calling you back for an interview. You're putting in the effort to improve a relationship; but, you're not seeing results.

My friend, God's not telling you no - He's just saying not yet. If you'll stay in line, be patient, and wait your turn; you'll overcome your struggles and accomplish your dreams. Be diligent in your waiting. Let your roots bear good fruit. Let your thoughts be right concerning the matter. Have no worries for your future. You have favor my love: "You shall flourish as a branch."

Stay in line in order to arrive on time. Otherwise, you'll experience delays on your journey; delays which could've been avoided with the help of patience. Wait your turn: as the sun waits behind the clouds to shine at its brightest; like a seed waiting to be watered to grow in beauty; like the rivers wait till overflow to rush. My friend, wait for the door to open.

When you find yourself playing the waiting game; consider your opponent and study him well. Take this time to study and become proficient in skill. Take this time to make the hearts of your neighbors glad with good word. Take this time to plan that business you always wanted to start. Take this time to get organized. Yes. And for those who need it - rest.

I beseech you my brothers and sisters of the call: remain steady and upright. You shall be delivered out of trouble. Let the beast pass and he will not bite you. Step on his tail and even your bones he will consume. Remember this when you're being taunted with insults and negativity. Don't give into their ways.

My friend, you have to wait for the meal to be prepared before you can eat it. In the same way, you have to wait on your blessings. Instead of being impatient, use this time to improve your attitude. The correct attitude is: "I may not be able to see much progress; but I know It's about to be my turn."

Stay in Line

People give up their turn by getting out of line. They give up on hope. They give up on love. They give up on themselves. And they give up on *The* Great Spirit. If only they could see into their future. If only they knew how close they were to their turn. But it doesn't matter now. My friend, get back in line. Wait. Don't let it happen again. Don't take the scenic route. You're so close. Yes. You're closer than you think you are. Stay in line.

I know the waiting is difficult. Your arrival seems impossible. Constantly, you've been faced with disappointment in life. You feel betrayed. Those whom you've loved the most have hurt you the most. My friend, hold your head up high. Don't be ashamed. It's about to be your turn. Be patient. Wait. Yes. Stay in line.

Don't give up on your dreams because things don't seem to be going your way. They'll never go *your* way. Not even *your way* is your way: all ways belong to God. My friend, you want things to happen on your time. *The* Great Spirit doesn't perform on man's time. Man's time is an illusion. It's fake and flawed. God's time is perfect and always right for the moment.

It might look like you'll never get out of debt. It might look you'll never be able to afford that house. It might look like your relationships will never get better. But as told from our youth, "looks can be deceiving." Things aren't what they seem. You're closer than you think you are.

Stay in line. Do the best you can for you. We cannot change other people; but we can change our situation. Walking away from someone you love should never be easy; but, sometimes it's necessary. You can choose to love and stay; or, love and leave. If its love; no matter what choice you make: it'll always remain.

Why are you impatient? You have to get right within yourself first. After this that man will come. After this that woman will notice you. Don't get out of line to chase the harlot. She'll lead you to a trap. Her doors remain open at all hours of the night. Once you enter, the door will slam shut behind you. She comes from an evil bloodline. Her name is confusion; her sister is wicked, and her brothers are deceit and destruction.

My friend, *The* Great Spirit's protecting you. He's keeping you safe by seemingly holding you back. Be of good cheer. It's for your good. You cannot see the viper in the bush ready to strike. Your focus is all over the place. Be still. Listen. Yes. Be alert and ready for what's to come. This is when the viper strikes to commit suicide.

Hear me lights of this world; hear me givers of good gifts; hear me salt of the earth: you're protected. Stay in line. Wait your turn. My friend, wait on *The Great Spirit*. It won't be long. Continue your good doing. Be patient. Others waiting in line with you are hungry for righteousness: feed them with your lips. Others thirst for the truth: give them to drink from spirit. There are people standing in line with you naked and afraid: my friend, cover them with love. Do not be bothered by the wait. Go right on producing delicious fruit.

When the time is right, *The* Great Spirit will move things around in your life. He'll speed somethings up. He'll usher in unexpected gifts. He'll cause opportunity to stand in line with you. Wait your turn. Focus on where you are. No worries my love, your arrival will be sudden.

You may feel alone, hurt, betrayed, or stuck in a bad situation. Hold on a little while longer: it's about to be your turn. *The* Great Spirit's provided you with a *way in* and a *way out*. What you're bothered by today will not be there to bother you forever. You feel weak. You feel like your stomach's crawling out of your body in sickness. You feel trapped. My friends be of good cheer: God will save you from your trouble. Yes. He'll save you from distress. He'll preserve you: for you are counted amongst the blessed. Wait on *The* Great Spirit.

Don't worry about the people trying to cut in line. God's got you covered. They will not be able to take what truly belongs to you. These are the people that'll try to throw you off balance. My friend, they want you to fall. If you fall, they'll stand in your place and try to hide your existence. Remain true to your purpose my love. Let your light shine bright! Arise! For a light cannot truly be hidden by darkness. It bursts through the cracks. It burns holes in the coverings. It draws life unto it. Kings recognize its divine presence and bow themselves before it. Shine my love. Shine! Yes. In spite of it all, rise and shine. You'll be granted the favor of *The* King.

You're so close the enemy is desperate. He's running out of weapons to use against you. The others did not prosper. Now, he'll try to use his secret weapon. If you stay in line under the shield of God: no harm shall come to you. Deception shall be revealed before the traitor is able to stab you in the back. Distraction will be silenced when the giant arrives. Delays will strengthen you. Disappointment will encourage you. Discouragement will propel you forward. But my dear friend, beware of you against you.

Don't be your own enemy. Don't hold yourself back from good things: trying to hold onto the bad ones. Good is lasting. What's not good in nature is temporary. It comes and goes when it pleases - if you let it. When it has used you up; when it has drained you: it will be done. When you fall it will not be there to pick you up. However, when you get back up again it'll return for more of you. Give it nothing my love. Be done with it. It's not for you. You're meant to have constant love. You're meant to have constant joy. You're meant to have constant peace. You're meant to have constant overflow from *The* Great Spirit. Stay in line. Yes. Wait with grace.

Hope To A Friend Sunrise

My friends, be ready to go. It won't be long. You'll be there in no time. For now, you're needed where you're at. Someone's paying attention to what you're doing. Someone's watching you. Give them a good show. Be the example. Be the change. Be love. Embrace your turn when it comes.

You've been in a traffic jam for some time now. Stay in line. Wait for the head car to move. Don't take the detour. It's led me to some strange places. It's put me in harm's way. Yes. I've been to a dangerous place in darkness. Hallelujah! I thank God for being the light that shines from within me. Yes. I thank God for sunrise.

Hear me branches of the true vine; hear me chosen instruments; hear me saints; hear me fellow heirs - my friends. Arise! Stand tall. Hold your heads up high. Move forward. Get ready, be ready, and stay ready. Yes. Take your rightful place in line. Shine bright where you are. Be of good cheer. The wait's almost over. It won't be long. It's about to be your turn.

Arise! It's Time To Shine.

Coming Soon!

Hope

To: *A Friend*

Sunshine

In the **Series**

| Sunrise | Sunshine | Solar Magnitude | Sunset |

Stay Connected

www.sradams.com

Arise!

Thy Light Has Come.

111

Administer of Love S. R. Adams

www.ingramcontent.com/pod-product-compliance
Lightning Source LLC
LaVergne TN
LVHW051624080426
835511LV00016B/2167